Foreword

Formed on March 21, 1943, 617 Squadron was created for a specific purpose – to execute arguably the most daring and innovative air raid of World War II, against the dams in Germany's Ruhr Valley.

On May 16/17, 1943, just 133 courageous airmen, flying 19 aircraft specially modified by industry, achieved enormous physical effect, bolstered morale at home and had lasting political influence on allies and foes alike.

The raid required imagination and accurate intelligence. It relied on complex planning and consummate flying skill to deliver a weapon precisely and at great range.

Wing Commander Guy Gibson selected a core group of airmen that he knew would be able to perform at the very high level required. The assembled aircrew comprised British, Canadian, Australian, New Zealand and American airmen; the cost of two dams destroyed and one damaged was high – 53 men were killed and three made prisoner of war.

Number 617 Squadron continued to deliver precision strikes, often with specialist weapons, to the war's end. Through the Cold War it served with a variety of aircraft types, famously including the Vulcan, before equipping with the Tornado. In 1943, the Dambusters deployed a remarkable new weapon system designed specifically for the dams raid and in 2003 it launched the Storm Shadow cruise missile for the first time in combat.

Today, 617 Squadron is the UK's premier operator of fifth-generation airpower, flying the F-35B Lightning from RAF Marham and the Royal Navy's new aircraft carriers, HMS *Queen Elizabeth* and HMS *Prince of Wales*. As it did in 1943, the squadron continues to pioneer new technologies, tactics and techniques, deliver precision airpower and, for the first time in its history, a formidable air-to-air capability.

▲ Equipped with the F-35B Lightning, the Dambusters are no strangers to embarked operations. The squadron worked with HMS *Queen Elizabeth* as part of Operation Achillean in November 2022. **AS1 Natalie Adams**/© UK MoD Crown Copyright 2023

The dams raid epitomised ingenuity, immense bravery, superb flying skills and the will to overcome adversity. Wing Commander Guy Gibson VC led his team with great focus and utter determination and the qualities and values they displayed then are those that form the foundation of the RAF today.

Wing Commander Stew Campbell took command of 617 Squadron in 2022, just in time for its 80th anniversary year. The privilege and honour he feels in leading one of the best-known Royal Air Force squadrons at this special time is palpable. The dams raid is an iconic event in Britain's history and it is important that 617 Squadron 'The Dambusters' should be remembered and celebrated.

In its 80th anniversary year, 617 Squadron is working through its regular, demanding training schedule, preparing to return to sea later in the year and, as in 2013, placing operational commitment ahead of its will to celebrate – much of the squadron will be overseas on exercise in May.

While it is away, the memorabilia-decked halls of the Lightning Operations Centre at RAF Marham will continue their own quiet, private celebration of the Dambusters' heritage, a celebration that reflects the discrete, precise manner in which today's 617 Squadron delivers its world class capability.

Paul E Eden
Editor

▲ Marked for the squadron's 60th anniversary in 2003, this Dambusters' Tornado GR4 carries a pair of Storm Shadow missiles. The unit debuted the weapon in combat that year.
© UK MoD Crown Copyright 2023

Official Licensed Product. Intellectual property of the Secretary of State for Defence is used under licence

Front cover image courtesy of Airfix

Contents

06 Personal Perspective
New Zealander Les Munro was the last surviving dams raid pilot. He continued with 617 Squadron after the attack and provided his perspective on the operation

08 Barnes Wallis: From Airships to Swing-Wings
Ken Ellis describes the engineering career of Barnes Wallis, inventor of the Dambusters' 'bouncing bomb'

16 The 'Bouncing Bomb'
Robert Owen, Official Historian of the No.617 Squadron Association, describes the development of the Upkeep weapon used to breach the Möhne and Eder dams

22 The Lancaster: Harris's Shining Sword
Tom Allett recounts the origins, development and service career of Avro's war-winning Lancaster

36 The Leader: Wg Cdr Guy Gibson VC
Graham Pitchfork tells the story of 617 Sqn's first leader and hero of the dams raid

44 The Station: RAF Scampton
The Dambusters launched their most famous raid from RAF Scampton on May 16, 1943, adding a significant highlight to the station's illustrious history

50 The Raid: Operation Chastise
Robert Owen describes the planning, training and execution of the raid that breached the great Ruhr dams

64 Commonwealth Connection
Australian, Canadian and New Zealand aircrew flew on the dams raid alongside their British allies. Simon Muggleton tells the story of just one, Canadian F/O Robert Urquhart

68 After the Dams
The Dambusters continued with a series of iconic raids during World War II. During the Cold War the squadron stood nuclear alert on

DAMBUSTERS 617 SQUADRON | 5

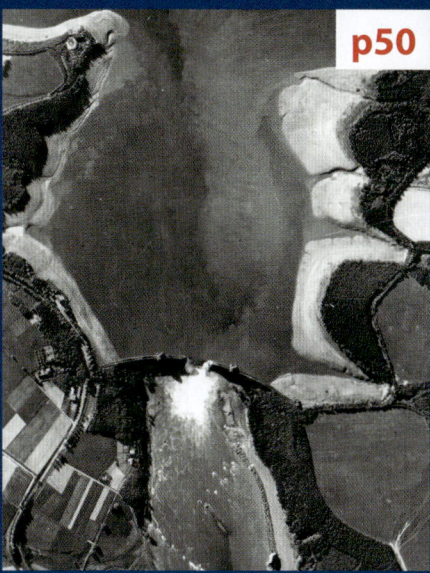

p36

p50

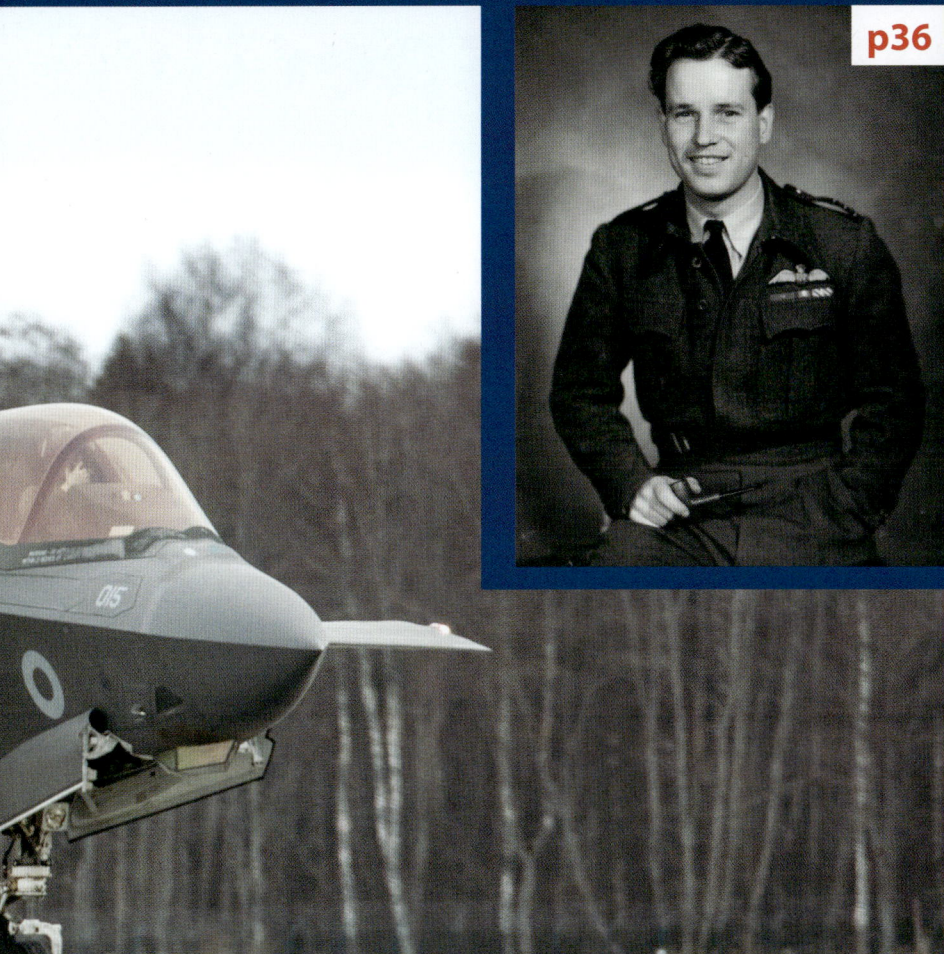

p104

p68

ISBN: 978 1 80282 713 2
Originally published 2013. Updated 2023
Editor: Paul E Eden
Senior editor, specials: Roger Mortimer
Email: roger.mortimer@keypublishing.com
Cover design: Dan Hilliard
Design: Steve Donovan, Lee Howson, Paul Sander
Advertising Sales Manager: Brodie Baxter
Email: brodie.baxter@keypublishing.com
Tel: 01780 755131
Advertising Production: Debi McGowan
Email: debi.mcgowan@keypublishing.com

SUBSCRIPTION/MAIL ORDER
Key Publishing Ltd, PO Box 300, Stamford, Lincs, PE9 1NA
Tel: 01780 480404
Subscriptions email: subs@keypublishing.com
Mail Order email: orders@keypublishing.com
Website: www.keypublishing.com/shop

PUBLISHING
Group CEO: Adrian Cox
Publisher, Books and Bookazines: Jonathan Jackson

PUBLISHED BY
Key Publishing Ltd,
PO Box 100,
Stamford, Lincs, PE9 1XQ
Tel: 01780 755131
Website: www.keypublishing.com

PRINTING
Precision Colour Printing Ltd, Haldane, Halesfield 1, Telford, Shropshire. TF7 4QQ

DISTRIBUTION
Seymour Distribution Ltd,
2 Poultry Avenue,
London, EC1A 9PU
Enquiries Line: 02074 294000.

We are unable to guarantee the bonafides of any of our advertisers. Readers are strongly recommended to take their own precautions before parting with any information or item of value, including, but not limited to money, manuscripts, photographs, or personal information in response to any advertisements within this publication.

© Key Publishing Ltd 2023
All rights reserved. No part of this magazine may be reproduced in transmitted in any form by any means, electronic or mechanical, including photocopying, recording or by any information storage and retrieval system, without prior permission in writing from the copyright owner. Multiple copying of the contents of the magazine without prior written approval is not permitted.

the Vulcan, before re-equipping with Tornado. Based at RAF Lossiemouth from 1994, it retired the Tornado and disbanded in March 2014, ready to reform on the F-35B

80 The Tornado: Swing-Wing Backbone
Withdrawn in 2019, the Panavia Tornado remained at the heart of the RAF's offensive capability for almost four decades

98 The Dambusters Today
Today, 617 Squadron flies the F-35B from RAF Marham. Officer Commanding 617 Sqn, Wg Cdr Stew Campbell provides a unique perspective on its operations and 80th anniversary year

104 Fifth Generation Dambusters
Wg Cdr Stew Campbell explains how 617 Squadron operates the fifth-generation, stealthy F-35B Lightning

The Personal Perspective

Les Munro was the last surviving dams raid pilot. He provided this personal perspective on the mission's 70th anniversary in 2013.

Seventy years ago in May, 617 Squadron created history by breaching the Möhne and Eder dams, and damaging the Sorpe. But at a cost. Eight Lancasters were lost, 53 aircrew lost their lives and three became prisoners of war. As I write, three of the 77 survivors are still alive today, Fred Sutherland in Canada, 'Johnny' Johnson in England and myself, Les Munro, in New Zealand.

This geographical spread reminds me of an opinion that I have expressed a number of times over the years when writing about 617 Squadron. It is that I believe that apart from the calibre of its aircrew, one of the strengths of the squadron was its cosmopolitan make up. That make up was certainly evident at its formation, but became rather more pronounced during what became known as the Cheshire era.

To illustrate, during the bulk of my time on the squadron it was commanded by Leonard Cheshire, an Englishman, 'A' Flight was commanded by Dave Shannon, an Australian, 'B' Flight by myself, a New Zealander, and 'C' Flight by Joe McCarthy, an American in the Royal Canadian Air Force. Of all my time with the RAF during the war, I look back on that period serving under and with Leonard Cheshire, with the deepest sense of pride and satisfaction.

What's the target?

But I digress. During the first few evenings, as those of us selected by Gibson, or selected by Group Headquarters, or who had volunteered, gathered in the mess, discussion centred on what was the target so important that it warranted calling together such a group of experienced crews. Obviously it was something special and beyond the scope of a normal Bomber Command operation. In this respect I doubt that many of those gathered at Scampton had ever heard of Barnes Wallis.

And yet it was entirely due to his knowledge of aircraft and engineering that we were posted to Scampton to form a special squadron. Likewise none of us would have known of the trials and tribulation that Wallis faced in getting acceptance of his revolutionary design that would become Upkeep.

Barnes Wallis developed Upkeep based on certain criteria, such as method of attack, including the height from which it was to be released, point of release, speed of attack, and so on. As a consequence of those criteria, the decision was made that the attack would be carried out at low level, which in turn would require moonlight conditions, and the further decision was made that the complete flight from base to target and return would also be at low level.

This established the type of training that we were to undertake over the next six weeks. The two most important aspects of this training were the pilots becoming competent at not only maintaining a constant height while following the contour of the land, but judging when to gain height to clear obstacles on the path ahead, and the relevant crew members becoming proficient at visual identification of landmarks that approach very quickly at low level compared with at high level, when they can be seen for many miles ahead.

▲ Squadron Leader Les Munro photographed in 1945. **RAF (AHB)/© UK MoD Crown Copyright 2023**

During that period of intensive training, both day and night, the opportunity of developing close friendships was limited, but nevertheless we came to recognise and respect other's strengths and operational experience. There also developed a competitive spirit, particularly between the pilots, which on occasions resulted in low-level dogfights when two or three Lancasters arrived back in the vicinity of base at the same time, with one attempting to get on the tail of another. It was most interesting, since it demonstrated the manoeuvrability of the Lancaster. By the end of training and as the day of the operation approached, a strong sense of esprit de corps had developed.

Successful Operation

The result of the operation on May 16/17, 1943 made history, acknowledged worldwide, and as *Salute* demonstrates, it continues to be the source of books, magazine articles and discussion. In the early 1990s, much to the concern of surviving crewmembers, opinions were expressed in the media that the operation was not successful, that the end result did not justify the means, with the loss of eight crews.

I refute that. I maintain that the raid was very successful in the operational sense. Both the primary targets, the Möhne and the Eder were breached and the Sorpe damaged. It is acknowledged, of course, that the Air Ministry, in deciding that the dams should be attacked, did not appreciate that the Germans would be capable of repairing the breaches as quickly as they did and in that respect maybe the raid wasn't a complete success. But nevertheless, the breaching of the Möhne and Eder caused major devastation to infrastructure such as factories, roads, bridges, electricity installations and so on, and did affect the German war effort. And very importantly, I believe the result of the raid gave a tremendous boost to the morale of the British people, which was somewhat low at the time and it was certainly successful in that sense.

Unfortunately, my plane was hit by light flak when crossing the Dutch coast at the island of Vlieland and the memory of those few seconds has remained with me ever since. I can still see the line of breakers on the foreshore, with the dunes behind, as we first approached the coast and then the line of tracer on the port bow, which appeared to be floating in the air as we cleared the dunes before reaching the waters of the Waddensee.

Over the years, when asked about the part I played in the operation I have always felt a sense of disappointment that I did not reach the Sorpe, which was my target. However, I console myself with the thought that had I reached my target, mine may have been one of those crews that never came back. As on a few other occasions, Lady Luck may have played a part that night.

Post-Dams

Post-dams, the squadron went through a hiatus period ending with the disastrous operation on the Dortmund-Ems Canal and the loss of six crews out of nine over two nights, including George Holden, the squadron commander, and David Maltby, 'A' Flight commander. Morale took a bit of a blow as a result of these heavy losses. However, the mood soon changed following the arrival of Leonard Cheshire as the new CO. Unlike Guy Gibson, here was a man who related equally with the lowest ranked aircraftman and the most senior officer under his command.

Dissatisfied with the marking of 617's targets by the Pathfinder Force, Cheshire and 'Micky' Martin introduced a policy of low-level marking that proved highly successful, with the squadron becoming renowned for its results on individual targets.

After completing the highly technical and comprehensive Operation Taxable, the D-Day spoof, the squadron dropped the 12,000lb Tallboy for the first time on the Saumur tunnel, and then on its first daylight operations on the E-boat pens of Le Havre and Boulogne. Squadron Association members visited the Le Havre docks in 1983 and the sight of the massive blocks of concrete tossed in jumbled heaps as a result of the attack, demonstrated the immense power and destructive force of the Tallboy.

Despite the departure of Cheshire in July 1944, the squadron continued to operate with distinction under the leadership of 'Willie' Tait, with the sinking of the German battleship *Tirpitz*, in conjunction with IX(B) Squadron, almost on a par for achievement with the dams raid. And to complete a very long list of successful attacks on individual targets of importance, the squadron carried Barnes Wallis's 22,000lb Grand Slam for the first time on an attack on the Bielefeld viaduct in March 1945. This was Wallis's original concept of what would be required to demolish the dams when dropped from a height.

To conclude, I believe that I can do no better in summarising the contribution to the war in the air by 617 Squadron and by both Barnes Wallis and the aircrews under the leadership of Guy Gibson (just one operation), Leonard Cheshire, Willie Tait and Johnny Fauquier, but quote the following passage from the opening chapter, *Briefing*, of Paul Brickhill's *The Dambusters*: "Once I asked an Air Marshal what he thought 617 was worth, and after a while he said, 'Well one can't say, but I suppose they were worth ten other squadrons.' He pondered a little longer and added, "No, that isn't quite so. Ten other squadrons couldn't have done what they did, and then of course you've got to consider that inventor chap and that freak weapon he gave them. I suppose 617 was the most effective unit of its size the British ever had." ◉

▲ This incredible photograph was taken from Les Munro's Lancaster during a low-level training sortie. **Les Munro**

▲ Wellington fuselages at Brooklands, at the beginning of the assembly process. **Vickers via Ken Ellis**

▶▶ Wallis in his office during the early 1970s. **Ken Ellis Collection**

BARNES WALLIS
From Airships to Swing-Wings

Barnes Wallis is most remembered for 'bouncing' and 'blockbuster' bombs, but he was also a gifted aircraft designer. Ken Ellis describes his achievements

With a view of the boats on the River Medina at East Cowes, the office was far from boring. From 1908, Barnes Neville Wallis toiled at a drawing board for J Samuel Wright, a well-known Isle of Wight shipyard. Fascinated by engineering, particularly design, the 21-year old was clearly gifted, but unqualified and unfulfilled.

Working alongside him was H B Pratt, previously employed by the armaments and shipbuilding giant Vickers at Barrow-in-Furness, Cumberland. Pratt had worked on a 'framed' airship called Naval Rigid R.1 and had been outspoken about serious flaws in Britain's first airship of the type. Referred to as 'Mayfly', because the programme dragged on and on, the 512ft (156m) leviathan broke its back on September 24, 1911 before flight trials commenced. Britain's airship ambitions lay in tatters in the waters of the Walney Channel.

Rivalries with Imperial Germany were by now extending beyond the bitter and costly race to build larger and bigger-gunned warships. The military potential of the Zeppelin airships could not be ignored and so Vickers re-established its airship works at Barrow in 1913. By then, Pratt was with 'Slippery Sam' Saunders's renowned East

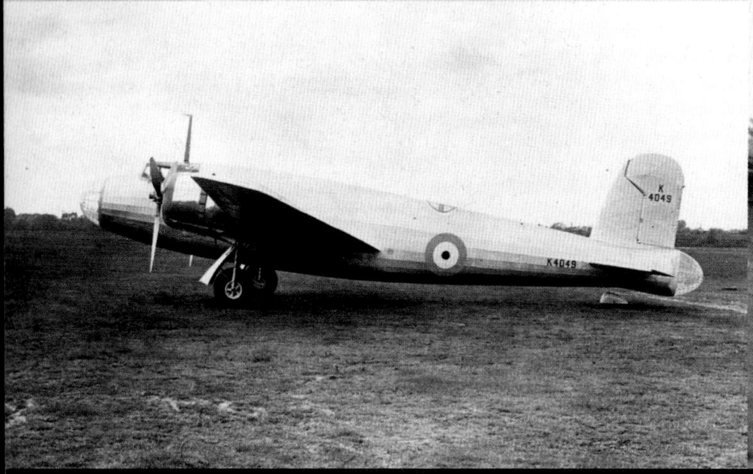

Cowes boatyard (and soon to be aircraft factory). Vickers wanted Pratt to head the new venture and he asked that Wallis join him.

The team set to work on R.9, but it was a political football, one minute in favour, the next teetering on cancellation. In March 1915 the axe fell and, disillusioned, Pratt and Wallis went off to enlist. Three months later the Admiralty re-adopted the project and the pair were ordered back, becoming Sub-Lieutenants in the process. R.9 first flew on November 16, 1916, but was underpowered.

Ships of the Sky

In September 1916 Zeppelin L.33 was captured more or less intact off the Essex coast and a pair of blatant copies, R.33 and R.34, were ordered, but not from Vickers. Barrow was running out of work, so a brand new airship, the R.80, was requested. In charge of this challenging commission was Barnes Wallis, aged 29.

From the start, R.80 was a standout design. Superbly streamlined and efficient, it could cruise at 65mph (104km/h) and carry a bomb load of 1,840lb (834kg) 3,800 miles (6,115km).

Along with Commander E A Masterman, Wallis created a mooring mast that revolutionised the operation of airships, especially in high winds. A coupling in the nose allowed the airship to dock with the mast, which swivelled into wind, then the craft could be secured using ropes. This was far faster than the previous haphazard, labour-intensive method.

R.80 development was drawn out, however, and the airship did not fly until July 19, 1920. It flew little and was scrapped in 1924. With no work coming his way, Wallis took a degree in engineering in 1922 and dabbled for a while with teaching.

Convinced there was a future for commercial airships, Vickers formed a subsidiary, the Airship Guarantee Company (AGC), to respond to a government requirement for an airship to fly to Canada and India. AGC received a fixed-price

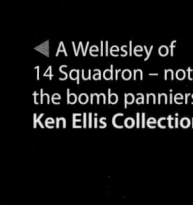

◀ A Wellesley of 14 Squadron – note the bomb panniers. **Ken Ellis Collection**

◀ The Vickers G.4/31 contenders, biplane and monoplane, displaying at Hendon in 1935. **Vickers-Armstrongs via Ken Ellis**

◀◀ The prototype Wellington at Brooklands. **Ken Ellis Collection**

▼ R.100 was an advanced design, far superior to the R.101, but it was killed off by the latter's failure. **Ken Ellis Collection**

▼▶ A Wellington Mk I awaiting its outer wings, but well on the way to completion. **Vickers via Ken Ellis**

contract for the R.100 in October 1924 – £350,000 (£19.25 million in present-day values), with swingeing performance penalties. Meanwhile, the Royal Airship Works at Cardington, near Bedford, was told to proceed with the R.101, without any such restrictions.

Wallis was back in demand. R.100 took shape at Howden, on Humberside. Among his team was Nevil Shute Norway, as a stressman. Norway went on to form aircraft manufacturer Airspeed and, as Nevil Shute, wrote novels, including *No Highway* (presaging the Comet jetliner disasters) and *A Town Like Alice*. At 709ft (216m) long, R.100 was huge, powered by six 670hp (499kW) Rolls-Royce Condors and could carry 100 passengers.

Despite its bulk, R.100 was exceptionally sleek and said to have had the lowest possible aerodynamic resistance for its cross-section. Weight saving was the mantra, with much use of duralumin and careful placing of load-carrying zones. Wire-mesh was used to keep the 15 gas bags in place and it was reported that this criss-crossing, and the rigidity it brought for little weight, inspired the geodetics that became the hallmark of Wallis's fixed-wing creations.

Cardington's R.101 was the first airborne, on October 14, 1929; it was underpowered, over engineered and massively expensive. Sixty-four days later, R.100 followed and showed immediate promise. It departed on a faultless flight to Canada in the summer of 1930, but on October 5, 1930, R.101 crashed into a hillside near Beauvais, France; seven people miraculously survived, 47 perished. Britain's airship era was terminated; R.100 was dismantled in October 1931.

End of the Biplane

Wallis had no need to look for work, the chairman of Vickers and its subsidiary, Supermarine, Sir Robert McLean, was determined to turn his talents to fixed-wing aircraft. He hoped that Wallis and his other 'young gun', Supermarine's Reginald Joseph Mitchell, would hit it off and provide new and vigorous approaches to Air Ministry specifications. The normally tolerant Mitchell, eight years Wallis's junior, took exception to Barnes, however, and there was a famous moment when they took separate trains to head office to explain that they could not work together.

McLean initially offered Wallis the post of head of structures. But then he upped the ante; Wallis was to work alongside chief designer R K 'Rex' Pierson at Brooklands. Having cut his teeth on types like the Vimy bomber, Pierson was the stalwart creative influence at Vickers. Pierson recognised Wallis's genius and was happy to accept his appointment. Their co-operation was to take the aviation division of Vickers from promising sideline to industrial dynasty.

The first type that Wallis worked on was the M.1/30 torpedo biplane, employing duralumin for its spars, longerons and fuselage stringers. Vickers had a reputation for big, robust biplanes and while the M.1/30 looked the part, it was actually much more radical than it seemed. It first flew on January 11, 1933, but on November 23 it broke up in the air, while carrying an inert torpedo. Test pilot 'Mutt' Summers and observer John Radcliffe successfully 'took to the silk'.

During the summer of 1931 the Air Ministry had issued Specification G.4/31 for a general purpose, light bombing and torpedo-carrying type to replace Fairey »

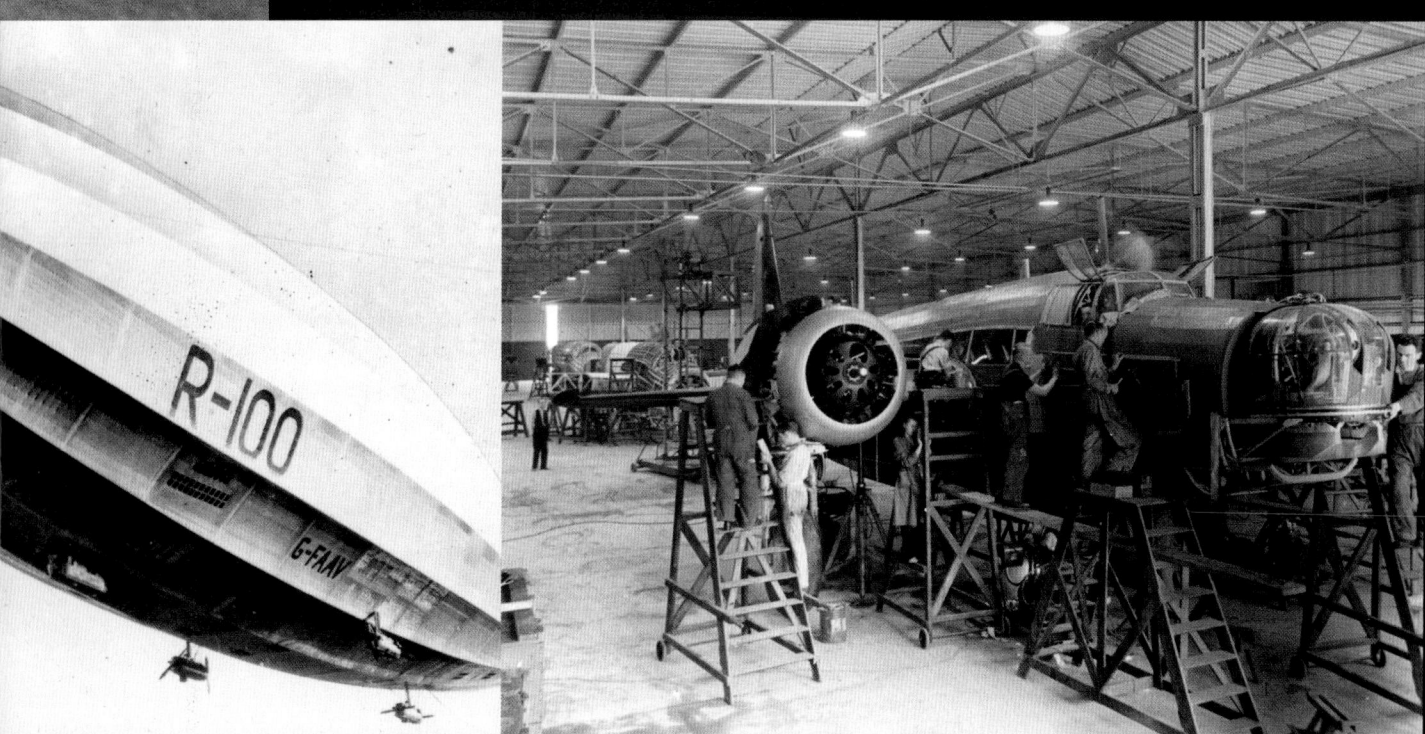

Gordon and Westland Wapiti biplanes. In depression-ridden Britain, the winner of this contract was looking at security. No fewer than nine companies – Armstrong Whitworth, Blackburn, Bristol, Fairey, Handley Page, Hawker, Parnall, Vickers and Westland – built prototypes for a fly-off. All were expensive gambles with nowhere to go if rejected.

There was a great temptation to 'play safe' with G.4/31 and stick to Pierson's proven formula, which had created the successful Vildebeest and Vincent biplanes, then in production. Nevertheless, McClean was inspired by Wallis and his new construction technique, geodetics, which looked set to produce lighter, stronger airframes.

Geodetics produced a lightweight 'basket-weave', providing exceptional strength. Tests at the Royal Aircraft Establishment Farnborough found that the new structure exceeded all previous requirements by a significant margin. The geodetics formed a strong outer structure that could adopt considerable curvatures and internal fittings, floors, etc. could be added as the airframe progressed down the production line.

Not only were geodetics light and durable, they were also easy to construct and repair. (Mitchell's Spitfire, by comparison, was also light and strong, but a nightmare to mass-produce.) Then, as its Wellington design was being finalised, Vickers stunned the Air Ministry by announcing in 1937 that, if ordered in hundreds, one bomber every 24 hours could be produced.

For the G.4/31 contender, a compromise was reached. It featured classic Vickers biplane characteristics but the fuselage, designed by Wallis, used geodetics for its 'shell', with conventional light alloy longerons. Wallis had also sketched monoplane layouts to meet G.4/31 and insisted that the time had come

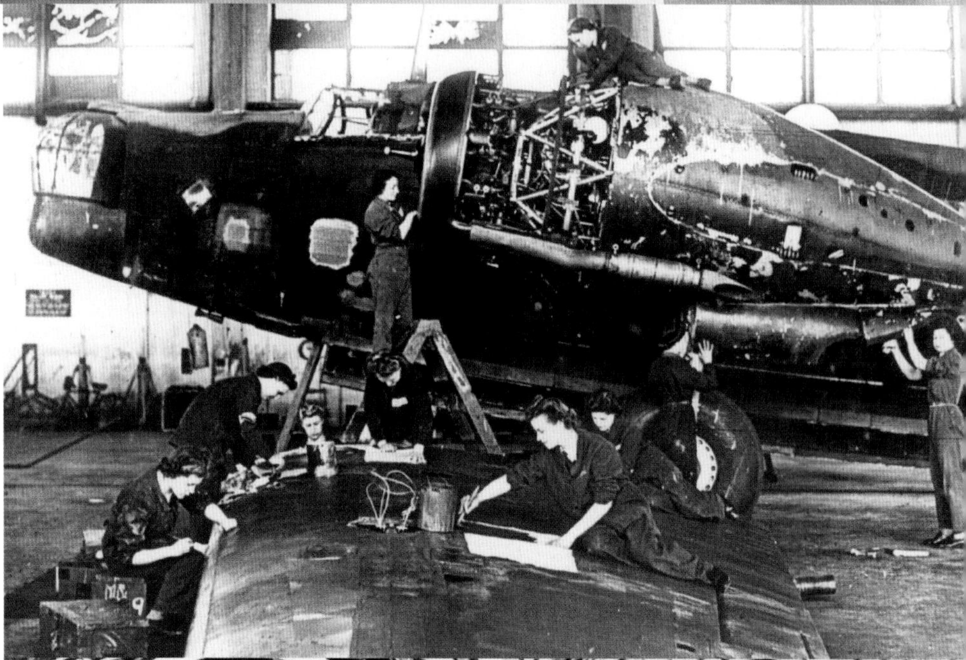

▲ Looking towards the tails of a pair of Wellington fuselages on the production line – the example on the right has the pilot's floor and seat in place. **Ken Ellis Collection**

◀ The Valetta general transport, typified by C1 VL249 shown here, and the Viking airliner capitalised on the Wellington legacy. **Vickers-Armstrongs via Ken Ellis**

◀◀ A Warwick GRI in D-Day markings and carrying an airborne lifeboat. **Key Collection**

◀▼ The Wellington's construction technique allowed it to take considerable battle damage. This all-woman Civilian Repair Organisation team was at work for benefit of the camera. **Ken Ellis Collection**

▼ The last geodetic bomber, the Windsor prototype. **Key Collection**

Often confused as external fuel tanks, the Wellesley carried a detachable pannier under each wing for up to 2,000lb (907kg) of bombs. These were needed because the 'egg shell' nature of the geodetic structure prevented large interruptions – such as bomb bays. (An egg is very tough, provided it keeps its shape.) By the time Wallis designed the Wellington, however, he had realised that large apertures could be made in the airframe without compromising its integrity.

Decisive Bomber

While the Wellesley contract was important for Vickers, it had a greater purpose as a pathfinder for another Air Ministry requirement of massive potential and, ultimately, vital strategic importance. Specification B.9/32 was seeking a twin-engined medium bomber to transform the RAF's offensive capability. Ministry parameters changed as the design rolled on, but Pierson and Wallis were not just ready for these, they were ahead of them.

Trevor Westbrook was given command of creating the new bomber en masse and worked with Wallis to standardise the geodetic sections so that there were fewer variations, and made them lighter still. By thinking beyond the prototype, Vickers made sure the bomber would enter service smoothly and quickly. This made the 'one-a-day' claim a far from idle boast.

On June 16, 1936 test pilot 'Mutt' Summers took the Vickers Type 271 for its maiden flight at Brooklands. Also on board were Wallis and Westbrook; the consequences of a disaster during that first circuit do not bear thinking about. Two months later, 180 were ordered, long before the official RAF evaluation.

At this point, the Type 271 was to be called Crécy, after Edward III's victory over Philip VI »

to drop biplanes. He got his way. A board meeting of April 12, 1932 decided to build both a biplane and a monoplane, at huge cost.

The biplane first flew at Brooklands on August 16, 1934. It was the victor of the hard-fought competition and the Air Ministry ordered 150 units. Hard on its heels was the monoplane, which took to the air on June 19, 1935.

That month, the two G.4/31s flew together at the Hendon Air Pageant and it was clear that the monoplane represented a huge leap forward. As well as this realisation, the mid-1930s showed that the 'G' for 'general purpose' was an anachronism. The big-span Vickers monoplane had the makings of an interim bomber and the other roles envisaged in G.4/31 were forgotten. The contract was re-issued in October 1935 and eventually 176 aircraft were delivered.

Long-legged General

Just 43 days after its maiden flight, the monoplane crashed on landing at Brooklands, thankfully without injury. The opportunity was taken to rebuild it to production standard and it re-appeared by the end of the year. The new bomber was named in honour of the brilliant soldier Arthur Wellesley, who became the first Duke of Wellington after his dazzling defeat of Napoleon at the Battle of Waterloo on June 18, 1815.

The first production Wellesley was delivered to 76 Squadron, RAF, at Finningley, Yorkshire, in April 1937. Eventually, six UK-based and four East African squadrons flew Wellesleys. The type then hit the headlines, with a non-stop flight from Egypt to Australia in November 1938. Two of the three aircraft that set off reached Darwin after 48 hours in the air, having flown 7,158 miles (11,520km). During the early phases of World War 2, the type also gave good service in action against the Italians in East Africa.

on August 26, 1346. That battle changed the face of warfare, with English longbows decimating the French forces under Philip's command. By September 1936, however, it was clear that the new bomber was very likely going to fight alongside France and it was renamed Wellington. The name of one of Britain's greatest field marshals had graced two aircraft in quick succession. Better to remember the man who had put paid to a demagogue with world-dominating ambitions in a Belgian field, than an overwhelming defeat on French soil!

The Wellington's contribution to Bomber Command was crucial; it took the brunt of the offensive until the four-engined 'heavies' gained momentum. At that point, its contribution was far from over, having already carved an important niche with the Operational Training Units, as a bomber in the Middle East and with Coastal Command.

On October 13, 1945 at Squires Gate, Blackpool, the last-ever Wellington, a Mk X, rolled off the production line. A grand total of 11,460 had been created, far more than any other British bomber. Wellingtons retired from RAF service, as crew trainers, in 1954, bringing to an end an astounding career.

Geodetic Legacy

Hard on the heels of the Wellington specification, the Air Ministry issued B.1/35 for a bomber that could broadly be called the 'Super' version of the earlier machine. The prototype Warwick first flew on August 13, 1939, but was bedevilled with a slow gestation as its powerplant, role and abilities were altered. From January 1943 it was assigned to air-sea rescue and became a very successful long-range saviour. Potentially a Wellington replacement, the Warwick was long out-lived by its elder relative.

With the Wellington in hand, 'bouncing' bombs and then the series of huge, high-velocity weapons increasingly absorbed

Early Days

Barnes Neville Wallis, second son to Charles and Edith, was born at Ripley, Derbyshire, on September 26, 1887. His father was a doctor but when Barnes was five, financial constraints brought the family to London. Barnes was educated at Christ's Hospital, a school that took gifted students who were not in a position to pay for tuition. Wallis did well at Christ's, but was without a qualification when he left.

His first job was with Thames Engineering at Blackheath; a 'jobbing' sub-contractor taking one-off contracts where it could. While some of the projects were interesting, including early vehicles, Barnes's quest for design opportunities kept him looking elsewhere. In 1908 he joined the shipwrights J Samuel Wright at East Cowes on the Isle of Wight. There he met with H B Pratt who had worked on the abortive 'Mayfly' airship at Barrow. Pratt and Wallis were destined to work on the R.100 airship, the beginnings of Wallis's aeronautical career.

▲ Airship R.100 at Howden, moored to the mast developed by Wallis and Masterman. **Ken Ellis Collection**

▶ Barnes Wallis with a model of the Swallow WCA in the mid-1950s. The starboard wing is in fully swept configuration, the port wing in the landing position. **Ken Ellis Collection**

▶▶ Early Wellington Mk IC P9249, issued to 38 Squadron at Marham in spring 1940. **Vickers via Ken Ellis**

Wallis's time, although his fertile brain had not abandoned aircraft; he would make a return with typically revolutionary ideas. 'Rex' Pierson oversaw the Warwick and the four-engined follow-through, the Windsor. During 1942 Pierson and Wallis talked through the possibility of an enormous six-engined bomber, intended to deliver a huge amount of ordnance, but not to risk as many precious aircrew. This was referred to as the 'fifty-ton bomber' and sketched in canard (main wings to the rear) configuration as well as a more conventional layout.

The last Vickers piston-engined bomber employed the large proportions that geodetics permitted, with high aspect ratio, elliptical wings. Characterised by its four-unit main undercarriage – one in each engine nacelle – the first Windsor flew on October 23, 1943. It was a monster, carrying a 12,000lb (5,443kg) bomb load, had a maximum all-up weight of around 60,000lb (27,216kg) and a span of 117ft 2in (35.71m). Avro's Lancaster had become the weapon of choice for Bomber Command, however, and only two more Windsors were built.

In 1945, Pierson became chief engineer and George Edwards took over the Vickers design department. The mother lode of the Wellington's legacy was not yet expended; Edwards knew that Vickers had to get into the civilian marketplace if it was to survive.

On June 22, 1945 the Viking airliner, its wings showing its Wellington ancestry, had its maiden flight. From this stemmed the Valetta military transport and the Varsity crew trainer, but the Viking's main claim to fame was to provide the bridge to major airliners. George Edwards (later Sir George) conceived the world-beating Viscount, taking Vickers to the VC10 and, through the British Aircraft Corporation, to Concorde.

Mach 4 to Australia

Wallis returned to aircraft by rekindling a desire for long-range commercial aviation that had its roots in the days of the R.100 airship. Travel at high speed to Australia was his goal, but he was experienced enough to know that such a radical concept would be impossible unless a military application could be found to share the investment.

Those who probe the life and times of Barnes Wallis beyond the R.100, the Wellington and the Dambusters, will note that he invented the 'swing-wing', or variable-geometry (VG) aircraft. This does the great man a disservice, because others were also alive to that aerodynamic solution and what Wallis was proposing was a re-invention of the aeroplane.

Using Messerschmitt design studies 'inherited' from a tunnel deep in the Austrian Tyrol in 1945, America's Bell Aircraft began work on the world's first VG aircraft, the X-5 jet. Capable of 'swinging' its wings from 20 to 60 degrees, this machine first flew on June 20, 1951.

What Wallis was proposing was first given an airing in a paper he presented in December 1948, entitled *Future Developments of Air Power*. Here, he came up with the term Wing-Controlled Aerodyne (WCA) as he believed that for supersonic, long-range flight, established norms of aerodynamics and format were obsolete. Wallis was talking of things called ichthyoid bodies – how fish morph to maximise their performance – and not a million miles from the dynamics that created an airship, or a bunker-penetrating bomb.

To achieve shapes capable of multiple-Mach figures, Wallis wanted to be rid of tail surfaces, to turn wings into the only control device and make 'fuselages' capable of a lift and/or control function. For this the wings would swing, but not just to allow for a combination of reasonable take-off and landing speeds with high-speed transit, as was the X-5's intent. Hence he wanted to talk of aerodynes, not aeroplanes.

What followed was one of Britain's longest research projects, running from 1950 to 1959. Given that most such ventures were aborted with great frequency in the 1950s, this was all the more remarkable. Using remotely controlled, trolley-launched scale models, Vickers followed two lines of development. Codename Wild Goose explored the swing-wing format, while Green Lizard investigated a point-defence system, using what today would be called a folding-wing munition. Both were tested at a specially built launch facility at Predannack, Cornwall.

Wallis hung on to his main aim throughout, the Swallow high-Mach, long-range airliner. At one point US defence money was ingested, but the project ran out of practical applications and petered out in 1959. In many ways Wallis was what he had always been – way ahead of his time. High-Mach aircraft are still a rarity and only in the 21st century have aerodynamicists talked of morphing airframes.

Knighted in 1968, Wallis retired from the successor of Vickers, the British Aircraft Corporation, three years later. Typically, he kept working on a series of projects, never abandoning his long-cherished ultra-fast, very long-range airliner. In August 1974 the prototype Panavia Tornado flew, and although it was not an aerodyne, a British swing-wing aircraft must have been pleasing to him. Sir Barnes Wallis died on October 30, 1979, aged 92. He would have enjoyed knowing that in January 1983 the Dambusters, 617 Squadron, began operations with a high-speed, swing-wing jet.

THE 'BOUNCING BOMB'
Developing the Upkeep Weapon

Identifying dams as potential targets was one thing, but attacking and destroying them was going to be considerably more difficult. **Robert Owen**, Official Historian of the No.617 Squadron Association, explains

▼ Flight Lieutenant David Maltby and crew flew ED906 on May 16/17, 1943. The aircraft remained with 617 Sqn, retaining its Upkeep gear even after further modification to take a 12,000lb Tallboy. Here the aircraft is seen on Scampton's Station Flight. **RAF Scampton Archive/© UK MoD Crown Copyright 2023**

▲ The Upkeep 'bouncing bomb' mounted on Wg Cdr Gibson's aircraft. The drive system to the right of the installation spun the weapon backwards before dropping.
RAF (AHB)/© UK MoD Crown Copyrigh 2023

The major dams of interest to the British were located to the east of Germany's heavily defended industrial area. They were small targets, difficult to locate and, as time progressed, likely to be increasingly protected. The task of attacking them was further complicated by the need to strike under cover of darkness. Costly daylight attacks during 1939 had forced Bomber Command to switch to night operations and its aircrew faced a steep learning curve as a result. The pre-war RAF had paid little attention to night flying, and aids for this, and navigation, were rudimentary.

Concerns over the accuracy and effectiveness of night bombing led to an investigation and in 1941 a report concluded that only one in ten crews claiming to have attacked the target got to within 5 miles (8km) of their objective. The chances of navigating accurately to a small target were slim, although the development of navigational aids would facilitate this task as the war progressed. Even having reached it, accurate bombing would be required and early World War II bombsights lacked the necessary precision. To compensate for this, aircraft dropped sticks of several small bombs in the hope that by straddling the target, at best one might hit, or at least be a near miss.

Therein lay a further problem. At the beginning of the war the RAF's main general-purpose bomb was the 500-pounder. A bomb of such weight, even if it scored a direct hit, stood little chance of causing catastrophic damage to a dam built with a masonry structure more than 100ft (30m) thick at its base, designed to withstand significant pressure and with a sloping face that would generally result in only a glancing blow.

Accuracy against such a target could be improved by mounting a low-level attack, possibly with torpedoes, although any target was likely to be protected by anti-torpedo netting, and the risk posed by the target's anti-aircraft defences was significantly increased. Regardless, it did not change the fact that all existing bombs were simply insufficient to cause critical damage to a dam.

Early Thoughts

Suggestions were made to overcome this fundamental failing. Might a number of bombs dropped from low level in the same place achieve cumulative effect? A number of bombs with delay fusing timed to detonate simultaneously might also be a solution, but such fuses were unreliable and imprecise. Accurate timing would be impossible to achieve, as would countermining – using a final bomb »

▼ Considerable modification was required to match the Lancaster BIII to Wallis's Upkeep weapon. With the bomb bay doors removed, the bomb and its mounting were left exposed inflight, leading to the loss of at least one Upkeep when it hit the sea at low level.
RAF (AHB)/© UK MoD Crown Copyright 2023

▼ Mosquito BIV DK290/G was involved in Aeroplane & Armament Experimental Establishment Highball trials. Here the aircraft has two of the weapons in its modified bomb bay. **Key Collection**

Highball – The Ship Buster

Once Wallis had determined the nature of his 'spherical torpedo', the development of an anti-shipping weapon, Highball, progressed in parallel with Upkeep. Containing a 600lb (272kg) charge and spun at up to 1,000rpm, Highball would bounce over the water towards its target, overcoming any torpedo defences. Striking the side of a vessel it would sink, clinging to the hull, to detonate beneath the unarmoured keel.

A smaller version of the weapon was successfully trialled by the Wellington at Chesil Beach. Production was soon in hand, the first Highballs being delivered in March 1943, with de Havilland Mosquitos modified to carry two in tandem. The weapon was intended to equip two squadrons, one in Britain and the other in the Mediterranean. Although the second did not materialise, the first, No.618 Sqn, was formed on April 1, ostensibly as an 'anti-submarine' unit and commenced training, flying from Skitten and Turnberry in Scotland.

To ensure neither weapon was compromised, Upkeep and Highball were to be used within hours of each other, with an attack (Operation Servant) against the German battleship *Tirpitz* in Alten Fjord due for the day before the attack on the dams.

While 618 Sqn trained in Scotland, trials were conducted at Reculver, co-incident with those for Upkeep. Between April 13 and 29, 23 wooden-skinned Highballs were dropped, revealing concerns about casing strength. Reinforced Highballs were released overground against armoured walls, leading to the further development of steel-cased weapons.

Trials against a target ship, the *Courbet*, moored in Loch Striven, commenced on May 9, but half of the weapons were lost due to release problems. These difficulties, and delays in the delivery of modified aircraft, resulted in the cancellation of Servant, although development continued in an effort to produce an operationally effective weapon.

By July 1943 problems were being resolved and successful double drops made. Further trials with steel-cased weapons at Reculver were promising. With no operation likely in the near future, however, in August 618 Sqn was briefed for anti-submarine operations using Highballs stripped of their casings, as cylindrical depth charges. It was a stopgap measure; the following month the squadron placed its modified aircraft in store.

Trials continued, including further attacks against the *Courbet*, and bouncing Highballs into railway tunnels. An air turbine was developed to spin the weapon and two Grumman Avengers were modified as carriers.

Now a viable anti-shipping weapon, it was not until June 1944 that a plan was devised for Highball's use in the Pacific against the Imperial Japanese Navy. Number 618 Sqn re-commenced training and in October, equipped with aircraft modified for carrier operations, it was despatched to Australia. There the squadron waited in vain for operations that never materialised.

Details of Upkeep and Highball were passed to the Americans and Russians, and a Douglas A-26 Invader was modified to carry Highball. It was destroyed during trials, when a bouncing weapon hit its tail. Highball development continued until 1947, its final installation being developed for the de Havilland Sea Hornet.

▲ The Highball installation was very obvious from below. **Key Collection**

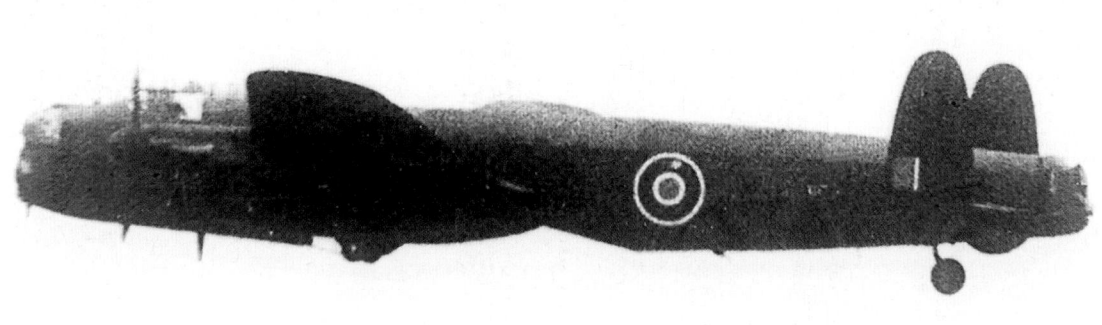

▲ ▶ Upkeep trials were flown off the Kent coast at Reculver, with the live weapon drop resulting in a massive spout of water. **both Gordon Swanborough/Key Collection**

to detonate them all – and could they be placed with sufficient accuracy in any case? Perhaps simultaneous attacks on both the water and air sides of the dam (using armour piercing bombs) might serve to undermine the foundations? All methods had their difficulties and there seemed no ideal solution. In any case, opinion varied as to how much explosive would be required to breach a dam.

Discussions begun before the war were still in progress in 1940. There seemed only one solution – a specialist weapon was required. Several ideas were proposed, including a self-propelled hydroplane, dropped from low level to skim over torpedo nets, or a glider torpedo used as a stand-off weapon to deliver a 2,000lb (907kg) charge. A number of such weapons might be detonated in the same place.

Development began, but the schemes received little official support and all foundered. Meanwhile, Barnes Wallis, Assistant Chief Designer (Structures) at Vickers Armstrongs, had begun investigating a means of destroying sources of the enemy's industrial power, including dams.

Wallis's initial idea had been to develop a large 10-ton (10,160kg) bomb, which, released from 40,000ft (12,192m), would penetrate the ground alongside a target and detonate at depth. Dropped into the reservoir close to a dam, the shock waves would cause a man-made earthquake that would shatter the objective. Since no current aircraft could carry such a load, Wallis also proposed a six-engined Victory bomber for the task. At this point, with neither production capacity nor materials to build such weapons available, the concept was rejected.

With typical tenacity, Wallis set out to determine exactly how much explosive would be required to breach a dam. The Road Research Laboratories at Harmondsworth, Middlesex and Building Research Station in Garston, Hertfordshire, constructed 1:50 scale models of the Möhne dam, which had been singled out as an important strategic target as early as 1937. Scale charges representing a 10-ton bomb were detonated in the water at varying distances. The results were not encouraging. Any water between the charge and the dam served to damp the force of the explosion.

To check the validity of these results, a larger scale experiment was conducted in May 1942 against the redundant Nant y Gro Dam in the Elan Valley, near Rhayader, Wales, calculated to be one fifth the size and strength of the Möhne. Results of the first test, with detonation at a distance from the wall, suggested that it would take a bomb of at least 30,000lb (13,608kg) to cause a breach. The turning point came in February 1942, however, when a technician unofficially detonated a smaller charge in direct contact with the wall, resulting in instant destruction.

The question was how to place such a charge so that it would sink in contact with the wall and detonate at the required depth? Conventional high-level bombing was still not accurate enough. Low-level attack would remedy this, but there was the danger that the bomb might bounce off the target before exploding. The charge required was too great for a torpedo, and in any case, the Möhne was protected by twin torpedo booms.

A Blinding Flash

Wallis was never able to explain quite how he came across the idea, denying that it came in a blinding flash: 'it took weeks, months'. But gradually he formed the idea for a weapon which, dropped from low level, would strike the surface of the lake and travel to the dam in a series of diminishing leaps. Striking the dam, it would sink in contact with the wall. To develop this, he needed to establish a law of ricochet.

Devising a suitable catapult and working in his garden, he fired his young daughter's marbles across the surface of a water-filled tin bath, seeking to determine the necessary criteria to achieve a controlled bounce. He then scaled up his experiments, shooting projectiles of varying shapes and densities across Silvermere Lake, near Cobham, close to the Vickers Works at Weybridge. From these he concluded that a sphere was the most suitable shape.

By mid-May 1942 he had produced a paper entitled *Spherical bomb, surface torpedo*, describing how a weapon using this principle might be used to attack a dam. At this stage he omitted any reference to backspin, which if imparted to a sphere, would generate lift, thereby lengthening the weapon's airborne path after release, ensuring that it struck the water at an angle of less than seven degrees, which was essential for ricochet. The spin would also lessen its impact with »

▼ The Möhne dam was attacked by bouncing the Upkeep weapon towards the dam wall.
RAF (AHB)/© UK MoD Crown Copyright 2023

▼ The Eder was a much more difficult target, its location in a steep-sided valley leaving crews with just seconds to line up and drop their Upkeep.
RAF (AHB)/© UK MoD Crown Copyright 2023

the water, and impart stability and accuracy during its run. Crucially, when the weapon struck the dam and sank, the spin would cause it to cling to the face of the wall. A hydrostatic pistol could be used to detonate the charge in contact at the most effective depth.

Experiments were then transferred to the National Physical Laboratories at Teddington. Here a ship testing tank, 640ft (195m) long, 23ft (7m) wide and 9ft (2.7m) deep provided controlled conditions. Wallis continued to fire 2in (51mm) diameter spheres of varying densities, made from materials ranging from lead to balsa wood, with different surface finishes – grooves, dimples and smooth. A sheet of steel lowered into the water replicated the dam wall and cameras filmed the surface and underwater behaviour of the missiles, which was just as Wallis had predicted.

Meanwhile, model tests were continuing to determine the minimum charge required to breach the Möhne dam if detonated in contact with the wall. A second test at Nant y Gro confirmed the results. Scaled up, a 7,500lb (3,400kg) charge exploded 30ft (9m) below the surface would produce a breach 50ft (15.2m) deep. As good as these results seemed, Wallis was being subjected to opposition as well as encouragement.

In July, the Director of Scientific Research and Development (Ministry of Aircraft Production) considered that dams were a hopeless proposition. At the end of September, Lord Cherwell, Churchill's scientific advisor was 'very unresponsive' towards Wallis, while Sir Henry Tizard, chairman of the Aeronautical Research Committee, was a strong supporter, recommending that Wallis should be asked to develop an 8,000lb (3,630kg) charge bomb for carriage by a Short Stirling or Avro Lancaster.

Wallis's supporters got their way, and by December 1942 a Wellington had been converted to carry 46in (1,168.4mm) diameter spheres, and a series of dropping trials began at Chesil Beach, Dorset.

Tripe of the Wildest Description
Initial drops were disappointing, the spheres breaking on impact, but varying height, speed and density over subsequent drops brought success. By February 1943, up to 22 bounces, and distances of 1,300 yards (1,189m) were being achieved.

Even so, Air Marshal Sir Arthur Harris, Commander-in-Chief of Bomber Command condemned the weapon as being 'tripe of the wildest description…' even though Wallis showed him film of the Wellington trials. On February 23, 1943, Wallis was summoned to the office of Vickers Chairman, Sir Charles Craven, and told to stop all work on the project. Wallis offered his resignation. But everything changed on February 26, when the decision to abandon the weapon was countermanded by instruction of Air Chief Marshal Sir Charles Portal, Chief of the Air Staff, who ordered development of a weapon suitable

Air Marshal Sir Arthur Harris, Commander-in-Chief of Bomber Command condemned the weapon as being 'tripe of the wildest description…'

for mounting an attack on the dams by mid-May. This left only eight weeks, and as yet no drawings for a full size weapon had been prepared, let alone one produced or tested.

Wallis was unable to obtain the steel for 79in (2,0007mm) diameter spheres suitable for carriage by a Lancaster (and to be known as Upkeep), so he created a 50in (1,270mm) diameter cylinder to carry the charge and padded this out, barrel fashion, with wooden staves. The first were dropped at a testing range at Reculver, Kent, on April 13, but the staves sheared off. Wallis ordered them to be tightened, but to no avail and after further unsuccessful drops on April 16 and 18, he decided to dispense with them and run the bare cylinder.

In this state, drops on April 21 and 22 were also failures. Reducing the release height from 150 to 50ft (45.7 to 15.2m) on April 29 brought success, repeated the following day. By May 2, Wallis had sufficient data to calculate that when dropped from 60ft (18.3m), at 210mph (338km/h) and spinning at 500rpm, the cylindrical weapon would travel 476 yards (435m). Further trials bore this out and by May 11, ranges averaging 450 yards (411m) were being achieved with five or six bounces.

To date the trials had only involved inert weapons, but a fully armed, Torpex filled weapon was dropped from 75ft (23m) off Broadstairs on May 13. Bouncing seven times, it covered 800 yards (732m) and sank before detonating at a depth of 30ft (9m), sending a plume of water 1,500ft (460m) into the air. Two days later, another was dropped, without spin, from 500ft (152m) to ensure that it would not be detonated by a hard impact with the water. All went well. Upkeep was ready to go to war.

Future Applications?

Following the success of the dams raid, other targets were sought for Upkeep. These included canals, viaducts, beach defences and anti-tank walls, for which the weapon was given a forward spin for overground travel. Trials were undertaken during July and August 1943 at Ashley Walk in the New Forest. They were successful, although stones and dirt thrown up by the bomb peppered several aircraft.

However, aiming remained a problem, as did devising a means of getting the weapon to explode on impact with the target, before it bounced off or carried on past it. These issues were never satisfactorily resolved. Other plans for attacking Italian dams in support of the invasion of Italy were cancelled for political and practical reasons. Thus, despite its success against the German dams, Upkeep never again bounced in anger. Nevertheless, seen as a potentially formidable weapon, its design and principles of operation remained an official secret until 1962.

LANCASTER & MOSQUITO
LIVE EXPERIENCE DAYS & TAXY RIDES

Ride in the aircraft and take part in an experience day with us that you'll never forget as you step back in time on our wartime airfield.
Lincs Aviation Heritage Centre…. where the emotions and exhilaration of warbirds await.
Now booking 2023 dates!

We are restoring the Lancaster to airworthy condition, get in touch for details on how you could support the project!

www.lincsaviation.co.uk   01790 763207
enquiries@lincsaviation.co.uk   East Kirkby Airfield, East Kirkby, PE23 4DE

THE LANCASTER
Harris's Shining Sword

Developed from the flawed Avro Manchester, the Lancaster went on to become Bomber Command's weapon of choice. **Tom Allett** describes the famous aircraft's evolution and service career

▲ In 2013 the Royal Air Force Battle of Britain Memorial Flight's Lancaster was marked as DV385/KC-AA 'Thumper Mk III', a 617 Sqn aircraft from June 1944.
Richard Paver

▼ Bomber Command began the war with a collection of largely unsuitable aircraft. These included the Hampden, the first of which for No.49 Sqn is shown here at Scampton. RAF Scampton Archive/© UK MoD Crown Copyright 2023

In the early stages of World War II, Britain's bomber force largely consisted of twin-engined, medium-capacity aircraft types including the Armstrong Whitworth Whitley, Handley Page Hampden and Vickers Wellington.

As the air battles in the night skies over Europe intensified and the operational limitations of these aircraft came to light, the Air Ministry sought a new generation of bombers that could fly further, higher, faster and with a bigger bomb load than their predecessors. It invited companies to put forward designs for a twin-engined medium bomber capable of carrying a bomb load in excess of 8,000lb (3,630kg), which was a considerable weight for the day. In reality, if such an aircraft could be produced, it would certainly warrant a 'heavy' designation.

Lancaster Evolution
Avro's Chief Designer, Roy Chadwick, already had a similar design project underway and responded by proposing the Avro Type 679 Manchester. With its vast bomb bay capable of carrying a wide range of armaments, the Manchester showed early promise. But it had an 'Achilles' heel' – its engines. Though powerful, its Rolls-Royce Vultures were plagued by unreliability to the extent that at one point in the aircraft's service career more aircraft were being lost to engine problems than combat damage. Even before that low point, however, it was obvious that a rethink was needed.

Legend has it that as he stood on the factory production line with some of his design team, Chadwick pointed up to a Manchester's wing and said: 'I want you to cut [the wing] here and here, and stick four [Rolls-Royce] Merlins on it". This revised aircraft, with a longer wing span, was originally designated Manchester B.Mk III, but in essence it was the first Lancaster. Carrying the serial number BT308, it was still officially referred to as a Manchester, but the documentation authorising its first flight designated it as a Lancaster.

Avro test pilots Sam Brown and Bill Thorn completed its first flight on January 9, 1941, and this was followed by a short but intensive series of test sorties. These were deemed successful and the Lancaster was soon on its way to the Aeroplane and Armament Experimental Establishment (A&AEE) at Boscombe Down for service trials. The second prototype Lancaster, DG595, was effectively the first production-configured airframe and the third machine, DT810, fitted with Bristol Hercules radial engines, became the prototype Lancaster BII.

The finished design had a flat-sided fuselage with a heavily-framed cockpit canopy sitting on top of, rather than partially enclosed within, the forward fuselage, like that of its Handley Page Halifax rival. Defensive gun turrets were mounted in its nose, tail and upper rear »

▼ DG595 was effectively the Lancaster Mk I production prototype. It featured the FN 64 ventral gun turret of the early machines, which was unpopular and often removed in service. **Key Collection**

fuselage, while the main undercarriage legs and wheels were housed inside the cowlings of the two inner engines.

The Lancaster's standard Main Force Bomber Command crew comprised seven members. The bomb aimer would normally be seated in the nose turret, except when guiding the pilot to his target, when he would lie down behind the Perspex dome beneath the turret. The dome provided its occupant with the best view from any Bomber Command aircraft of World War II, especially from 1943, when larger blisters were fitted. Although bomb aimers were not officially authorised to be in their 'working' position below the turret during take-off, many chose to sit or lie there anyway.

Behind and slightly above the bomb aimer – positioned almost side-by-side – were the pilot (there was no co-pilot) and flight engineer, the latter sitting on a fold-down seat. The navigator's table, facing to the port (left) side was immediately behind them and, just a few feet further back, the wireless operator sat on the left-hand side of the fuselage, facing forwards. The loneliest positions were those of the mid-upper and rear gunners who were both separated from their crewmates along the fuselage.

At the time the Lancaster was evolving from the Manchester, the war was going badly for Britain and its allies. Weapons introduced during wartime often suffer from being rushed into service by some degree, and, with the enemy seemingly dominant on all fronts, the pressure to push the new four-engined type into service must have been enormous. Perhaps the most notable

▼ The Manchester entered service with a triple-fin tail arrangment, which later gave way to a more effective design with the twin fins and rudders that were subsequently used on the Lancaster. The change made little difference to the Manchester's overall suitability to role. **Key Collection**

Lancaster Mk I Specification
Type: heavy bomber
Powerplant: four 1,640hp (1223kW) Rolls-Royce Merlin 22 inline piston engines; Merlin XX or 24 also fitted
Performance: maximum speed 287 mph (462km/h); ceiling (loaded) 19,000ft (5,793m); range (loaded) 2,530 miles (4,072km)
Weights: empty 36,900lb (16,738kg); maximum take-off 70,000lb (31,751kg)
Dimensions: wing span 102ft (31.00m); length 69ft 4in (21.08m); height 20ft 6in (6.23m)
Armament: up to 22,000lb (9,988kg) of bombs, plus two 0.303in (7.7mm) Browning machine guns each in the nose and mid-upper turrets, and four 0.303in or two 0.5in (12.7mm) Browning machine guns in the tail turret

adjustment the Lancaster required after entering RAF service was the introduction of strengthened wingtips after airborne failures were suffered at high operating weights. Nevertheless, overall, the Lancaster BI was a very successful design that required few airframe refinements.

Power and Production

In order to keep up with demand for the hugely successful Rolls-Royce Merlin engine that powered several Allied aircraft types, it was license-built in the USA. The American engines were known as Packard Merlins and used in the construction of over 3,000 Lancasters, which were designated as B.Mk IIIs, though the airframe itself was essentially identical to that of a BI. A limited production run delivered 300 B.Mk II aircraft, equipped with Bristol Hercules engines owing to a temporary shortage of Merlins.

British-built Lancasters were manufactured by various companies at several locations: Avro at Chadderton (near Manchester) and Yeadon (Leeds); Metropolitan-Vickers at Trafford Park (Manchester); Armstrong-Whitworth at Coventry; the Austin Motor Company at the Longbridge car manufacturing plant in Birmingham and by Vickers-Armstrongs factories at Chester and Castle Bromwich (Birmingham).

Among the aircraft built by Austin Motors were a number of B.Mk VII machines that were immediately recognisable because they carried a mid-upper turret of revised layout. Known as the Martin turret and positioned slightly further forward on the fuselage than the regular Frazer-Nash installation, it was electrically driven and equipped with two 0.5in (12.7mm) machine guns rather than the 0.303in (7.7mm) weapons of the Frazer-Nash.

In Canada, Victory Aircraft in Malton, Ontario, built the B.Mk X, which was essentially a BI airframe with Packard Merlin engines and North American-style instrumentation and electrics. However, later examples of the Victory-built aircraft also had the Martin turret.

Into Combat

The Lancaster entered RAF service with No.44 (Rhodesia) Squadron, which took delivery of its first aircraft on Christmas Eve 1941. No.97 (Straits Settlements) Squadron followed suit soon afterwards. After a conversion course from the Manchester that sometimes consisted of just a single flight for the pilots, but only the chance to study the aircraft's instruction manual for the rest of the crew, 44 Squadron was ready for combat duties by the early spring of 1942.

The first Lancaster operation was a mine-laying trip to Heligoland Bight, carried out by four aircraft from 44 Sqn on March 3, 1942; all returned safely. The first true bombing raid involving the type was against the German city of Essen on the night of March 10/11, 1942. This time 44 Sqn provided two aircraft, each carrying 5,000lb (2,270kg) of incendiaries; both Lancasters returned safely.

Harris's Influence

The Lancaster's debut had occurred just one month after Bomber Command had received a new Commander-in-Chief, Air Marshal (later Marshal of the Royal Air Force) Arthur Harris, and his appointment led to a complete transformation of the force. He immediately set about lobbying the British Prime Minister, Winston Churchill, to increase the size of his bomber force and was ultimately successful.

In 1942, with the Allies deemed too weak to mount an invasion of continental »

The Hercules-engined Mk II was more powerful than the Mk I, but could not match the Merlin aircraft for speed or altitude. The Hercules radials also made for a more 'draggy' installation, increasing fuel consumption.
Key Collection

▼ The Stirling flew alongside the Halifax and Lancaster with Bomber Command, but was always inferior to the later types. This Stirling Mk I was at RAF Scampton.
RAF Scampton Archive/© UK MoD Crown Copyright 2023

Europe in the near future, the only way to forcefully carry the fight to Germany was via the Allies' bomber force. Before Harris's arrival, Bomber Command was trying – and failing – to make a significant contribution towards Britain's war effort by striking specific industrial targets, including factories. Despite the bravery of the bombers' crews, their primitive navigational aids were unable to make up for the basic fact that they could not see small targets in the dark.

With Churchill's support, Harris turned Bomber Command's strategy away from attempting precision attacks, towards a policy of area bombing. The number of aircraft, squadrons and airfields available to the Command increased rapidly and over the next three years it was transformed into a very powerful and effective fighting force, capable of devastating German cities.

The timing of Harris's new strategy was perfect for Avro and as its new machine began to win friends among RAF crews, the company was in the right place at the right time to step up production. Initially, many airmen converting to the Lancaster from either the Short Stirling or Handley Page Halifax, said they believed the Avro machine's physical strength and general build-quality to be inferior to their previous types. That perception was short-lived, however, and the type went on to win almost universal praise from those who flew it.

Growing Capabilities

The basic Lancaster airframe was used on many different tasks during the war, including mine laying and anti-submarine operations. However, it was its role as Bomber Command's primary weapon for Main Force operations, deep into Germany, through the last three years of the conflict that sealed its place in history.

Harris developed several ideas for increasing Bomber Command's effectiveness, including the 1,000 Plan, his desire to place an unprecedented number of bombers over a selected target in a single

Lancaster Production Statistics	
Prototypes	2
Mk I	3,425
Mk II	301
Mk III	3,039
Mk VII	180
Mk X	430
Total	7,377

raid, delivering a hammer blow from which recovery would be very difficult. He put his theory to the test for the first time on the night of May 30/31, 1942.

Hamburg was selected as the target for the raid, under the codename Operation Millennium, but poor weather forced Cologne to be chosen as an alternative. Despite the fact that this raid was almost two and a half times larger than anything that had been attempted before, it came so early in the type's operational service that only 73 of the 1,047 bombers dispatched that night were Lancasters. Nevertheless, the 1,000 Plan was indicative of what lay ahead. Mass formations would be sent to overwhelm German night defences and the Lancaster's prodigious weight-lifting capabilities made it the ideal 'big stick' weapon.

The prototype Lancaster was authorised to fly at a maximum take-off weight of 39,000lb (17,690kg), while the second prototype was cleared to 60,000lb (27,216kg), and within months of the type's operational debut, Lancasters were regularly operating at weights up to 63,000lb (28,576kg). Bomb loads varied

▼ Groundcrew work to prepare this No.57 Sqn Lancaster for another sortie, possibly adding to the nine misisons recorded on its forward fuselage. The unit flew its Lancasters from RAF Scampton between September 1942 and August 1943, briefly operating alongside 617 Sqn.
RAF Scampton Archive/© UK MoD Crown Copyright 2023

according to the type and distance of the chosen target, but a mixture of munitions weighing up to 14,000lb (6,350kg) was routinely carried.

Unlike the RAF's other four-engined 'heavies', the Halifax and Stirling, the Lancaster was designed from the outset to carry the cylindrical 4,000lb (1,814kg) 'Cookie' high-capacity bomb, which had a thin metal casing to allow maximum blast effect. The subsequent coupling of two and then three Cookies together, allowed 8,000lb and 12,000lb versions to be created and the Lancaster was the only aircraft capable of carrying the latter.

With an increasing number of aircraft delivered, the type soon became the backbone of Main Force operations, with hundreds of Lancasters making almost nightly attacks against Germany's major cities and industrial centres.

Operational Equipment

Like all the RAF's heavy bomber types, the Lancaster was vulnerable to attack from its crew's blind spot underneath the fuselage. German night-fighter crews had learned to »

▲ The Lancaster's size, payload capability and versatility made it an ideal platform for test work. This machine flew post-war as an engine test bed with Armstrong Siddeley Motors. **Key Collection**

▲ The 4,000lb Cookie was an unimpressive weapon to look at, but highly effective against buildings. Its blast effect knocked down structures, while incediaries were often dropped at the same time, to light fires in the damaged buildings.

▼ Number 57 Squadron Lancasters prepare for take-off at Scampton. Ten of 57's Lancasters flew on the famous low-level attack on the Schneider factory at Le Creusot in 1942.
both RAF Scampton Archive/© UK MoD Crown Copyright 2023

▲ Modified to carry a droppable lifeboat, the Lancaster became an air-sea rescue platform as the ASR.Mk III. **Key Collection**

▲ Photo-reconnaissance was another Lancaster role. This PR.Mk I served 'B' Flight, No.541 Sqn in 1946. **Key Collection**

Main Force
From summer 1942, Bomber Command began using Pathfinder crews to precisely locate and mark targets. The Pathfinder squadrons were drawn from the regular bomber groups and from January 1943 they combined to form No.8 (Pathfinder) Group, better known as the Pathfinder Force.

The Pathfinders flew the same aircraft as the dedicated bombing squadrons, increasingly focussing on the Lancaster. They flew ahead of the bomber formations, which became known as the Main Force, representing, as they did, the primary thrust of Bomber Command's striking power.

▲ This RAF Battle of Britain Memorial Flight formation of Lancaster, Spitfire and Hurricane joined the flypast over Buckingham Palace to mark the 60th anniversary of VE-Day, the end of the war in Europe, in 2005.
SAC Scott Robertson/© UK MoD Crown Copyright 2023

◀ PA474 is the RAF Memorial Flight's Lancaster Mk I.
SAC Taylor/© UK MoD Crown Copyright 2023

down their opponents by concentrating fire at the aircraft's main fuel tanks, situated between the fuselage and engines.

However, the battle for supremacy in the night skies over Europe was more than a duel in the dark between crews; it was also being 'fought' between Allied and Axis scientists in the safety of their laboratories. Both sides developed combat aids and countermeasures as the night air war became increasingly intense.

British bombers received 'Monica', more properly known as ARI 5664, a radar system with its aerial located under the aircraft's rear turret. While it initially proved successful in alerting bomber crews to approaching enemy fighters, the Germans soon developed a passive airborne radar device that enabled Luftwaffe fighters to home in on Monica transmissions.

Similarly, while the H2S radar fitted in a Perspex dome underneath the rear fuselage of all RAF heavy bomber types by 1943 greatly enhanced Bomber Command's navigational accuracy, it also emitted a signal that Luftwaffe fighters could home on. This device and countermeasures 'race' continued throughout the war, with H2S radar pulses later being used to develop Fishpond, another night-fighter warning system that was monitored by the bomber's wireless operator.

Lancaster Legend
The so-called battles of Berlin, Hamburg and the Ruhr are just three of the prolonged battles of attrition that were spearheaded by Lancasters, but away from its usual area bombing role, the type flew two unique raids that will always be held up as outstanding examples of precision bombing and derring-do.

The first, which took place little more than a month after the Lancaster had been declared operational, was a daylight raid against the MAN Diesel engine factory in Augsburg, Germany. MAN built engines for Germany's U-boat fleet and 'Bomber' Harris wanted to see if his new aircraft was capable of striking high-value precision targets deep inside enemy territory. Attacking the MAN factory required a round-trip in excess of 1,000 miles (1,600km), which at that time made it the longest daylight deep penetration raid into Germany yet attempted.

On the afternoon of April 17, 1942, 12 Lancasters, six each from 44 and 97 Sqns, took off from their Lincolnshire bases for the daring low-level attack, flew almost due south to cross the coast at Selsey Bill, descended to just 50ft (15m) across the English Channel, then thundered over farmers' fields en-route to Augsburg.

Enemy ground and air defences hit the two formations hard and only eight Lancasters succeeded in reaching the target. The factory was hit and significant damage caused, but only four of the 12 aircraft made it home.

Squadron Leader John Nettleton led the raid and his was the only 44 Squadron crew to return. For the courage and determination he displayed that day, he became the first of ten Lancaster airmen to win the Victoria Cross.

Of course, the Lancaster will always be associated with the Dambusters raid on the night of May 16/17, 1943. The crews who flew those straight and level attack runs in the dark, holding steady at approximately 60ft (18m) »

Master Bomber

On the night of May 16/17, 1943, Wing Commander Gibson exercised active control of the Lancaster attacks against the Möhne and Eder dams, setting a precedent for what became the Master Bomber concept. The possibilities for tight control of a raid's progress were further examined with some success during a June 21/22 attack on the Zeppelin works at Friedrichshafen, which were manufacturing Würzburg radar components.

The first major raid featuring a Master Bomber was flown against the V-Weapon research establishment at Peenemünde on the Baltic coast. The August 16/17 attack saw Group Captain JH Searby flying as Master Bomber, controlling the Main Force Halifax, Lancaster and Stirling bombers by radio, and meeting with considerable success.

▲ The RAF Memorial Flight's hangar at Coningsby is always busy outside of the display season, when the Flight's aircraft undergo deeper levels of maintenance. The Lancaster's copiously glazed bomb-aimer's position included an optically flat lower panel for the bombsight.

▼ Regular changes of nose art allow the RAF's Lancaster to commemorate various significant aircraft, squadrons and pilots. The '*PHANTOM OF THE RUHR*' artwork allowed PA474 to represent No.100 Sqn's EE139, which completed 121 operational missions.
both © UK MoD Crown Copyright 2023

and 230mph (370km/h) over the water while being shot at by the 20mm cannon defending the Möhne dam, arguably displayed the greatest feat of airmanship of World War II.

Another notable raid in which Lancasters played a leading role was the attack on the Nazi V-weapon development factories at Peenemünde, in August 1943. It marked the first Lancaster raid for the Canadian squadrons of No.6 Group and the first time that the RAF used a Master Bomber to coordinate an attack. The task fell to Lancaster pilot Group Captain John Searby, of 83 Squadron.

Heavier Loads
As the war progressed, the Lancaster's payload capabilities continued to increase. With their nose and mid-upper turrets removed and most of their defensive armour plating stripped-away to save weight, a few Lancasters were converted to carry a single 12,000lb (5,443kg) Tallboy or 22,000lb (9,979kg) Grand Slam deep-penetration bomb.

Though only used on a handful of occasions, the very high-value targets struck by these new weapons ensured that their employment created headlines. Numbers IX(B) and 617 Squadrons combined efforts using Tallboys, capsized the battleship *Tirpitz* in November 1944, and Tallboys and Grand Slams were also used with great effect against targets including U-Boat pens, V-weapon sites and railway viaducts.

Manna and Tiger Force
In the last few months of the war, as the Allied armies began to liberate most of Western Europe and RAF and USAAF fighters overwhelmingly dominated the airspace over continental Europe, Bomber Command largely reverted to daylight operations. In the last few days before the Nazi surrender the RAF planned and executed Operation Manna.

In a complete change from its usual attack role, Manna required the bomber force to drop food parcels to starving Dutch civilians in the then still-occupied parts of western Holland. Lancasters flew all of the 3,156 food-dropping flights undertaken before hostilities ended on May 8, 1945. This was achieved for the loss of only three aircraft; two in a mid-air collision and one through an engine fire.

By the end of the European conflict, Lancasters had taken part in almost 138,000 attacks, of which just over 35,000 were made in daylight. In October 1945 the RAF informed manufacturer A V Roe that the Lancaster had dropped well over 600,000 tons »

(609,628 tonnes) of bombs on primary targets, based on over 150,000 sorties being flown. At least 35 Lancasters are known to have completed 100 operational sorties, an incredible achievement considering Bomber Command's often punishing loss rate.

When the war in Europe ended it was originally envisaged that many Lancasters would continue to serve in a bombing role against Japan, as part of Tiger Force, which was being prepared for Pacific operations when the atomic bomb suddenly ended the conflict.

In all, 7,377 Lancasters were built. After the war the RAF retained a number as bombers and maritime patrol aircraft, until they were replaced by their Avro Lincoln and Shackleton descendants. A huge number of war-surplus Lancasters was offered for sale and the air arms of Argentina, Australia, Canada, Egypt and France all operated Lancasters until they were replaced by more modern types.

Another significant part of the Lancaster history is that, as the Avro Lancastrian, aircraft converted to carry passengers played a significant part in opening up the world's post-war long-haul air routes. In 1946, a Lancastrian operated by British South American Airways flew the first scheduled flight from the new London Airport, known today as Heathrow.

However, the greatest tribute to describe the type's achievements was that made by 'Bomber' Harris. After the war, when Lancaster production was coming to an end, he wrote to the production group's management saying:

▼ Post-war the Lancaster still represented a useful and readily available military capability. The Royal Canadian Air Force was among its operators. **Key Collection**

"As the user of the Lancaster during the last three and a half years of bitter, unrelenting warfare, I would say this to those who placed that shining sword in our hands.

"Without your genius and your effort, we would not have prevailed – the Lancaster was the greatest single factor in winning the war." »

▲ Battle of Britain Memorial Flight Lancaster PA474 emerged from major servicing in 2017 with its left side marked to represent 'L-Leader', a 460 Sqn, Royal Australian Air Force machine, including distinctive nose art that reflected the multinational origins of its crew.
RAF BBMF/© UK MoD Crown Copyright 2023

Company Connections

During World War II, just as it did before the war and has ever since, the RAF relied on industry partners for the delivery of aircraft, equipment, support and, in the case of Operation Chastise, a specially developed weapon. Three British companies and one American company can be identified as the primary contractors behind the Lancaster aircraft and the Upkeep weapon employed on the dams raid.

Rolls-Royce designed the Merlin engines that powered the Avro Lancaster, although the aircraft chosen for modification to Type 464 (Provisioning) standard were Mk IIIs, equipped with engines built by Packard in the US. Meanwhile, Vickers engineer Dr Barnes Wallis was responsible for the extraordinary 'bouncing bomb'.

Avro

Alliott Verdon Roe flew his first aircraft in 1907, achieving a series of 'hops', but failing to achieve sustained flight. His next machine, a triplane, was far more successful, allowing him to become the first English pilot to fly in a British aircraft when he conducted successful trials with the type in 1909.

The pioneering pilot and designer registered A.V. Roe and Co on January 1, 1910, gradually expanding his 'Avro' business to include two factories and a flying school. Without doubt the company's most successful product of the period, the Type 504 biplane trainer appeared in July 1913 and remained in production until 1932. Nevertheless, the 1920s were generally difficult and in 1928 Roe sold his interest in Avro to JD Siddeley, who also had Armstrong Whitworth under his control.

Meanwhile, Sopwith, famous for the World War I Camel fighter, had been reborn as Hawker in 1920. The new company bought Gloster Aircraft in June 1934, and acquired Armstrong Siddeley and Avro in July. Under its Hawker Siddeley Group parent, Avro then produced the Anson reconnaissance, training, and transport aircraft; the Manchester; and the superlative Lancaster. Post-war, its most successful product was undoubtedly the Vulcan jet bomber.

Further acquisitions followed in the 1950s and Hawker Siddeley Aviation remained active until 1977, when it was forcibly merged with the British Aircraft Corporation and Scottish Aviation to form a nationalised aircraft manufacturer, British Aerospace (BAe).

On November 30, 1999, British Aerospace merged with Marconi Electronic Systems to create BAE Systems, which has itself grown through acquisition to rank among the top seven largest defence companies globally based on 2021 revenue. Its responsibilities to the UK Ministry of Defence include the production, support and ongoing evolution of the RAF's Eurofighter Typhoon and major roles in F-35 Lightning development, production, and support.

▲ This 617 Sqn F-35B was operating with HMS *Queen Elizabeth* as part of Operation Achillean in November 2022. BAE Systems is deeply involved in both Lightning production and support and is a partner in the Aircraft Carrier Alliance. © **UK MoD Crown Copyright 2023**

▲ In the beginning… A.V. Roe takes a passenger aloft at Blackpool in 1910. **Key Collection**

Alongside Babcock International, the Ministry of Defence and Thales, BAE Systems is also a key member of the Aircraft Carrier Alliance responsible for the design, construction, and support of the Royal Navy's Queen Elizabeth-class aircraft carriers.

Rolls-Royce

The Lancaster was schemed around a powerplant of four Rolls-Royce Merlin engines. Today, the company is responsible for or part of the manufacturing and support infrastructure for many of the RAF's aircraft propulsion systems, including the lift fan for the F-35B.

Its history goes back to 1884, when Henry Royce established an engineering business. In 1904, Royce built a car. In May he introduced it to Charles Rolls and between them they agreed to build and market a range of vehicles under the Rolls-Royce brand. In 1906 they formally launched the Rolls-Royce company and Rolls subsequently stepped back to pursue other interests, flying among them. In July 1910, he was killed after his aircraft broke up in the air.

Nonetheless, in 1914 Royce turned his attention to aircraft engines in response to an Air Department of the Admiralty request soon after the outbreak of World War I for

▲ The Rolls-Royce Merlin, or its Packard equivalent, powered the majority of Lancasters. **Key Collection**

Packard, which built the engines installed in Lancaster Mk III airframes, was primarily an automotive maker. It began trading in 1899 and began building Merlins in summer 1940; it had completed 55,523 by war's end. The original Packard name disappeared in the mid-1950s and although briefly resurrected, it had gone for good by the end of the decade.

Vickers

Vickers was established in 1828 and began manufacturing military equipment in 1890. By 1897 the company had acquired a shipbuilding interest and, as Vickers Sons & Maxim, it became a major supplier to the armed forces. It built an unsuccessful naval airship in 1901, but had more success in 1911, when it began manufacturing aircraft and teaching pilots how to fly them.

As an aircraft manufacturer Vickers produced several successful types during World War I, followed by a series of large airliners and RAF bombers through the interwar years. Late in 1928 it absorbed Supermarine, which later developed the Spitfire. The companies continued to trade separately, as they did in 1938, when they became part of the Vickers-Armstrongs Group. In 1960, Vickers was merged with elements of Bristol and English Electric to form the British Aircraft Corporation (BAC). In 1977, BAC and Hawker Siddeley were merged into BAe.

Vickers' shipbuilding interests had continued through changes of ownership and name, ultimately as GEC Marconi Marine, which became part of BAE Systems, responsible for submarine production, in November 1999.

a new 200hp-class engine. The company's debut aeroengine, the Eagle, was an outstanding success.

Subsequent engine designs cemented Rolls-Royce's position as Britain's pre-eminent supplier of aircraft engines, a position that enabled the company to develop the superlative 'R' racing engines for a series of Supermarine floatplanes that ultimately won the Schneider Trophy outright for Britain in 1931. Royce died in 1933 but, by then, techniques and technologies pioneered in the 'R' engines were informing a new design, the Merlin.

Wartime development peaked with the Griffon and a new engine that reused the Eagle name, but was quickly overtaken by the gas turbine, or jet, in which Rolls-Royce was already invested. Post-war it forged a global presence in turbojet, turboprop and, later, turbofan production, before development issues with the RB211 forced it into liquidation. Purchased by the UK Government in 1971, the company was divided into separate automotive and engine enterprises in 1973 and in 1987 the latter was privatised.

Since then, Rolls-Royce has again established itself as a world leader, through independent projects and collaboration. Interestingly and of direct relevance to today's 617 Sqn, the engines powering the Queen-Elizabeth class aircraft carriers are manufactured by Rolls-Royce Marine.

▼ The Hawk T.Mk 2, represented here by aircraft marked for IV Sqn and flown by 25 Sqn instructors and students, was built by BAE Systems. The company is embedded in its day-to-day operational support, alongside Rolls-Royce and other contractors. **SAC Emily Muir/© UK MoD Crown Copyright 2023**

THE LEADER

Wing Commander Guy Gibson VC

Guy Gibson led 617 Sqn on the dams raid, winning a Victoria Cross in the process. As **Graham Pitchfork** explains, he was a courageous leader, but also a complex, difficult man. He died at the age of 26, when his Mosquito was shot down on 'just one more mission'

Born in 1918 the youngest of three children, Guy Penrose Gibson spent his early childhood in Simla, India before his mother returned to England with her children when Guy was six years old. He was later educated at St Edward's School, Oxford, where his progress could best be described as steady rather than distinguished.

At St Edward's he developed a keen interest in flying, but his first attempt to join the RAF was unsuccessful. However, with the RAF in the midst of a series of expansion schemes, creating a need to train more pilots, he re-applied and made the grade.

On November 16, 1936, he joined his fellow student pilots at Yatesbury to start his flying training. He was awarded his wings on May 24, 1937 and selected for bombers. After completing his advanced training in September 1937 he reported to 83 (Bomber) Squadron based at Turnhouse, near Edinburgh, to fly the biplane Hawker Hind. Considered over confident, and by no means modest, he did not make friends easily. Indeed, his groundcrew called him the 'Bumptious Bastard' and, later in his career, some of his aircrews gave him the nickname 'Boy Emperor'.

In the spring of 1938, the squadron moved to Scampton near Lincoln and a few months later re-equipped with the Handley Page Hampden. Although assessed as average, Gibson was passionate about flying and, unlike many of his colleagues, he was happy to fly in marginal conditions. He attended a navigation course where he was, once again, assessed as average, but his instructor, who clearly had considerable foresight, added 'could do well'.

On the day war broke out, six 83 Squadron Hampdens, including Gibson's, took off to find the German fleet, but bad weather and darkness frustrated the attempt. It would be almost six months before Gibson flew another operation.

With the German invasion of Norway on April 9, 1940, 83 Squadron was tasked to drop mines in the Kattegat and Skagerrak and Gibson flew his first operation on the 11th. Following the German Blitzkrieg into the Low Countries on May 10, the squadron was soon in action again and Gibson dropped his first bombs on Germany on the night of the 16th.

Throughout the summer of 1940 he took every opportunity to fly on operations, frequently volunteering to fly extra sorties and in July he was awarded the DFC. When he was not flying he led a hectic social life, centred on the RAF's favourite public houses in Lincoln and Nottingham. On September 23 he took off to bomb Berlin, a target at the maximum range of the Hampden, as part of the largest raid on the German capital at that stage of the war. Unlike some others, Gibson found and attacked his target. It was his 37th and final operation on 83 Squadron.

Pressing On

During his time on 83 Squadron, Gibson had made few friends and could be openly hostile to those that he considered did not have sufficient press-on spirit. However, his aggressive attitude to engage the enemy at every opportunity had been noted by higher authority, not least by the Air Officer Commanding (AOC) of 5 Group, Air Vice-Marshal Arthur Harris.

As Gibson started his rest tour at an Operational Training Unit (OTU), the German offensive against Great Britain had switched from day to night attacks and Fighter Command was short of experienced night pilots. AVM Harris was approached to identify some of his bomber pilots to transfer to Fighter Command. He obliged and Gibson was sent to 29 Squadron at Digby, near Lincoln, with a promise from Harris that he would get an operational command on his return to Bomber Command.

The squadron was converting to the Bristol Beaufighter IF, but success generally eluded its crews. Despite being newly married and with his wife living nearby, flying was more important to Gibson and he grabbed every opportunity to fly. With Sergeant Richard James as his air-intercept (AI) radar operator, he achieved his first kill late on the night of April 14, 1941 when a Heinkel He 111 was shot down off the Lincolnshire coast.

The squadron moved down to West Malling in Kent, and within days Gibson shot down his second enemy aircraft, on the night of May 3. Despite making numerous AI contacts, further success was elusive and Gibson did not hide his frustration and envy »

▲ Wing Commander Gibson and dams raid crews outside Buckingham Palace after receiving their decorations. Flt Lt 'Micky' Martin is to Gibson's right, Flt Lt Joe McCarthy at his left. **617 Sqn Archive/© UK MoD Crown Copyright 2023**

▶ Gibson poses in the cockpit of a No.83 Sqn Hampden at Scampton. **RAF Scampton Archive/© UK MoD Crown Copyright 2023**

◀▲ Guy Gibson with the original 617 Sqn badge, featuring the King's crown, inset. **both RAF (AHB)/© UK MoD Crown Copyright 2023**

▲ Gibson with his wife, Eve. **617 Sqn Archive/© UK MoD Crown Copyright 2023**

▶▼ AVM Cochrane, AOC 5 Group. **RAF (AHB)/© UK MoD Crown Copyright 2023**

▶ Gibson with 83 Sqn at Scampton. **RAF Scampton Archive/© UK MoD Crown Copyright 2023**

as his colleagues built up their scores. He did gain a third confirmed victim on July 6 when he sent a Heinkel 111 into the sea off Sheerness but, with Luftwaffe activity decreasing during the summer, it was to be his final victim and he grew increasingly impatient at failing to achieve further success.

It was during this period that he was given a puppy, a black mongrel that was mostly Labrador. In September, he was awarded a Bar to his DFC and, after a year on 29 Squadron, he was posted as the chief flying instructor to 51 OTU at Cranfield, an appointment he neither wanted nor enjoyed.

A Hard Taskmaster

On February 22, 1942, Air Marshal Harris was appointed AOC Bomber Command. Among a number of major initiatives, he wanted to introduce a more vigorous leadership and he remembered his promise to Gibson made a year earlier. By early April, Gibson had left Cranfield and was promoted to acting wing commander, to take command of 106 Squadron flying the Avro Manchester, but soon to convert to the Lancaster.

As a squadron commander, the youthful Gibson led from the front. He flew on the difficult operations, leading by example when his courage and determination to inflict the maximum damage on the enemy was never in doubt. He was a hard taskmaster and demanded the same level of commitment and professionalism that he made. He had little sympathy and understanding for those who did not measure up to his high standards and he would soon move these people on to other appointments.

With his upbringing in the Raj and at a British public school, he only felt comfortable with the officer class, in particular those who possessed the same level of press-on spirit that he displayed, men such as John 'Hoppy' Hopgood, Dave Shannon and his own wireless operator, Bob Hutchison. All would join him on 617 Squadron. He was never at ease with non-commissioned officer (NCO) aircrew and had little rapport with the groundcrew, many of whom disliked him. Yet, when the time came to write letters of condolences to the families of those who had been lost, this complex and intolerant man would often add his own personal paragraphs to those drafted by the adjutant. On a night when he lost three of his best crews he was grief stricken and their loss reinforced his grim determination to hit Germany even harder.

By his drive and determination, and his enthusiasm to engage the enemy, Gibson moulded 106 Squadron into one of the most effective Lancaster units. His efforts were rewarded when the squadron was selected to carry out a special operation, which Gibson led, with a new bomb, against some of Germany's capital ships thought to be at the Baltic port of Gdynia. Although the raid was a failure, here was the first instance of Gibson and his squadron being selected for special training with a new weapon.

Throughout the autumn of 1942, Gibson continued to fly on the most demanding sorties. In November he was awarded the DSO for his courageous leadership and inspiring example. On January 16, 1943, the noted BBC radio journalist, Richard Dimbleby, was Gibson's passenger when Bomber Command attacked Berlin for the first time in eleven months. Dimbleby's broadcast was a triumph and added to Gibson's growing reputation as one of Bomber Command's most effective squadron commanders.

After eleven months in command, he flew his 72nd and last bombing operation (29 with 106 Squadron). Shortly afterwards he was awarded a Bar to his DSO, when the citation recognised his 'contempt for danger'.

Gibson was summoned to see the AOC of 5 Group, AVM the Honourable Ralph Cochrane, who asked him, "How would you like to do one more trip?" Although exhausted and overdue for a rest, it was an offer that a man like Gibson could never refuse.

A New Squadron

He arrived at Scampton on March 21 to form 'X' Squadron, soon to become

617 Squadron. Contrary to popular belief, Gibson did not choose all his crews, but he did select a nucleus of pilots he knew and trusted, among them Hopgood and Shannon from 106 Squadron and Harold 'Micky' Martin.

Creating a new squadron to carry out a unique and unorthodox operation in just two months was a daunting and exhausting task. On March 29 he was told that the squadron was to carry out low-level attacks against dams, but it would be many weeks before he was able to inform his crews. He was introduced to Barnes Wallis, inventor of the Upkeep bomb, soon after arriving at Scampton. They were to establish a warm and close relationship in the weeks ahead.

Gibson concentrated on training his 21 crews to fly at very low level, initially in daylight and then at night. He drove the men of 617 hard and two crews failed to match up to the standard he demanded. He immediately had them posted to other units. Because of the very tight security that surrounded the impending operation, he was unable to disclose the reason for their training and this added to the intense strain placed on him.

As the date for the operation approached, Gibson continued to fly training sorties with his scratch crew, in addition to attending meetings, visits to watch trials of Upkeep and entertaining visiting VIPs, all of which placed greater pressure on him. With the exception of Hutchison, his wireless operator on 106 Squadron, he knew little about his crew and rarely mixed with them socially, particularly the NCO members, preferring the company of the small group of pilots in his inner circle. On May 11, Gibson dropped his first Upkeep, although not all crews were able to practise with the weapon before the operation.

The two primary targets for Operation Chastise were the Möhne and Eder dams, and Gibson selected his best crews for these, with others assigned to the Sorpe dam and the remainder acting as a back-up force. The date for the operation was set for the night of 16/17 May.

The Dams
The evening before the attack, Gibson was very weary after the pressures of the previous two months. His feet were painful as a result of a bout of gout but he refused painkillers, knowing that he would be flying the following night. During that evening his dog, a faithful companion for two years, was hit by a car and killed on the main A15 road alongside the station and he worried that some of his crews might consider this to be a jinx. The dog's loss deeply affected his lonely master. »

▲ AM Harris, soon after his appointment as AOC Bomber Command. **RAF (AHB)/© UK MoD Crown Copyright 2023**

▼ Gibson (centre) during his time as OC 106 Sqn, with John Searby to the left and Peter Ward-Hunt. Searby flew as Master Bomber on the August 1943 Peenemünde raid. **via Graham Pitchfork**

During the afternoon of May 16, he briefed his crews in the presence of Cochrane and Wallis. Shortly after 9.30pm he took off with Shannon and Martin and headed for Germany's dams at the culmination of weeks of intense training and pressure. Despite his exhaustion and fatigue, Gibson was able to call on his single-minded determination and self-confidence over the coming hours and he was confident of success.

Typically, he led from the start. Once he had gathered the survivors of his force near the Möhne dam, he made the first attack, dropping his bomb accurately. Hopgood followed him but was shot down as he crossed the dam. Gibson immediately joined the third aircraft (Martin) and flew parallel to him and slightly higher to draw the flak. He continued to counter the flak when the fourth and fifth aircraft attacked. This was a selfless and gallant act of a man who was determined that the perilous operation would succeed at all costs. After the Möhne was breached, Gibson led the remaining three Lancasters to the Eder as the others headed for home.

The Eder was a much greater challenge but it too was breached. Operation Chastise had been a resounding success, although the loss of eight aircraft and their crews was a very high price to pay.

The next morning Gibson and the survivors celebrated their spectacular success. Later in the day, two events typified much of Gibson's complex character. He investigated two early returns and the failure of another crew to deliver an attack. He exonerated the first two but was dissatisfied with the third pilot's reasons for failing to attack and he and his crew were immediately posted from the squadron. He then arranged the sending of the 56 telegrams to the next of kin of the missing and gave instructions that he would want personal letters to follow.

The success of the raid made Gibson into a national hero, but the anti-climax after so much effort, while mourning the loss of his friends, left him depressed. Even the announcement that he had been awarded the Victoria Cross and the news that HM the King would be visiting the squadron did little to raise his spirits.

Desperately in need of a rest, and as a national hero, there was no possibility of him returning to operations. Two months after the raid Gibson left for a tour of the United States. After three years of almost continuous operations, he found it difficult to settle into a more mundane existence.

Enemy Coast Ahead

On his return from the USA four months later, there were many who thought that his fame had gone to his head. He found little fulfilment in his marriage and his philandering was common knowledge. He »

▲ This photograph of Gibson was taken for the book *Air Aces*, by Gordon Anthony, first published in 1944. **RAF (AHB)/© UK MoD Crown Copyright 2023**

▶▼ Gibson and crew posed for this photograph with his dams Lancaster, ED932, after the raid. RAF Scampton Archive/© UK MoD Crown Copyright 2023

▼ The grave of Gibson's dog is immaculately maintained outside 617 Sqn's wartime hangar at RAF Scampton. Gibson's office window is above and right of the blue sign. **Flt Lt Sarah James**

The Last Survivors

Three of the men who flew alongside Gibson on May 16/17, 1943 survived to mark the 70th anniversary of the dams raid, but none remains to mark its 80th.

Les Munro

New Zealander Les Munro was the last surviving pilot. He had flown with 97 Squadron and at the end of his tour was awarded the DFC. He and his crew responded to a call for volunteers for a 'new' squadron to undertake a special operation.

For the dams raid, they were part of the northern wave of aircraft tasked to attack the Sorpe. Their aim was to fly at low level over the North Sea, to coast in near the heavily defended island of Vlieland. As they crossed the coast their Lancaster was hit by anti-aircraft fire, which severed the electrical system and the intercom and they were forced to turn back.

Munro went on to become one of the mainstays of 617 under the leadership of Leonard Cheshire. Munro was appointed as a Flight Commander and flew on many raids, including Operation Taxable, the spoof operation designed to simulate an invasion fleet off the Pas de Calais on the night of D-Day. He later dropped the new 12,000lb Tallboy bomb, but after a year on 617 Squadron he was rested. He was awarded the DSO, having completed 58 bomber operations.

Les Munro later commanded a Bomber Command Defence Training Flight, before leaving the RAF at the end of the war as a squadron leader and returning to New Zealand. He died on August 4, 2015, aged 96.

George 'Johnny' Johnson

George 'Johnny' Johnson trained as an air gunner and joined 97 Squadron in July 1942 as a 'spare bod'. He re-mustered as a bomb aimer and joined the crew of Joe McCarthy, an American serving with the RCAF. The crew participated on operations until March 1943, when they were selected to become part of 617 Squadron forming at Scampton.

McCarthy's crew was one of the two that successfully attacked the Sorpe, flying along the length of the dam and dropping their bomb without spin from the lowest possible height. Visibility over the target was poor and the crew spent half an hour perfecting their line of approach before releasing their bomb on the tenth run; although they were accurate, the dam was only damaged, not breached. Johnson was one of the 34 recipients of an award for this operation, receiving the DFM.

Following the dams raid he went on to complete a further 19 operations with 617 Squadron, before being screened (classed as 'tour expired' or, in effect, due for a rest from operational flying) and posted to a Heavy Conversion Unit. He remained an instructor until the end of hostilities. Post-war he served with 100 Sqn on the Avro Lincoln and later the Avro Shackleton with Coastal Command's 120 Squadron. After a period in the Far East he returned to the UK for a final tour, retiring as a squadron leader in 1962. He died on December 7, 2022, aged 101.

Fred Sutherland

Canadian Fred Sutherland joined the RCAF in July 1941 and trained as an air gunner. At OTU he crewed up with a young Australian pilot, Les Knight. In September 1942 they joined 50 Sqn, flying Lancasters. After completing around 30 operations they were posted to 617 Squadron.

Sutherland and his crew attacked the Eder during the epic raid. The two aircraft ahead dropped their Upkeep bombs but the dam remained intact. Knight, who had the last bomb, made a number of attempts on this very difficult target and eventually succeeded. It was a perfect attack and the dam wall was breached.

He and his crew remained with 617 and on the night of September 15/16, 1943 they were part of a force of eight aircraft detailed to attack the Dortmund-Ems Canal near Munster. It was Sutherland's 40th operation. In very poor visibility, their Lancaster hit treetops. Two engines were disabled and Les Knight had great difficulty controlling the aircraft, eventually ordering the crew to bale out. They all succeeded, but Knight was still at the controls when the aircraft crashed.

Sutherland had landed in Holland and headed south, making contact with a Dutch woman who fed him. He was passed from safe house to safe house and taken down the escape lines through France, before crossing the Pyrenees into Spain. After two months on the run he reached Gibraltar and was flown back to England. He did not return to operational flying and was repatriated back to Canada. He died on January 21, 2019, aged 95.

also appeared to openly criticise some of Bomber Command's tactics and this did not please Harris, his mentor. He was appointed to a number of unfulfilling tasks, which did nothing to assuage his restlessness. It was during this period that his classic book *Enemy Coast Ahead* was written.

His final months were not happy and his old failings of intolerance and pomposity resurfaced. He did not want to be left out of the fighting war and he felt marginalised. On the night of September 19, 1944 he flew a Mosquito on a raid to Rheydt. It has never been fully explained how he came to be on the raid, but for some time he had been lobbying both Harris and Cochrane to allow him to 'fly one more'. In the event, on the return from the target, flying at low level, his aircraft came down in Holland and he and his navigator were killed. Their remains were laid to rest in the cemetery at Steenbergen.

The loss of the 26-year old Gibson came as a great shock to the nation, to the air chiefs and to those who had flown with him. Sir Arthur Harris described him as a 'warrior' and of that there is no doubt. His operational record was unsurpassed and rarely equalled. Richard Todd's sympathetic and powerful portrayal of Gibson in the film *The Dam Busters* reinforced his legendary status and reminded the world of his outstanding qualities of leadership and courage. Despite his failings and weaknesses, when the time came to face the ultimate test, often in the face of the gravest danger, Guy Gibson never flinched from his duty.

▲ Gibson demonstrated his fearless determination during early operations on the Hampden. **RAF Scampton Archive/© UK MoD Crown Copyright 2023**

▲◀ RAF Scampton's Ethos and Heritage Centre has parts of the wreckage of the Mosquito in which Gibson was lost. **Paul E Eden**

▼ Pages from Wing Commander Gibson's logbook tell their own story. **Andrew Thomas**

Dambusters 617 Squadron 80th Anniversary 1943 -2023 Commemorative Badge

On the night of 16/17 May 1943, Wing Commander Guy Gibson led the Royal Air Force's specially formed 617 Squadron on an audacious bombing raid to destroy three dams in the industrial heartland of Germany.

AWARD is proud to commemorate the 80th Anniversary of the heroic 617 Squadron Dambusters Raid, code name 'Operation Chastise', with the exclusive Limited Edition Dambusters 617 Squadron 80th Anniversary Commemorative Badge. This highly collectable badge is sequentially numbered on the reverse, has been traditionally manufactured to the highest standards and comes in a personalised fitted presentation case with a hand numbered certificate of authenticity inlay card resulting in a very desirable commemorative to treasure and making a perfect gift.

- Strictly Limited Edition of 617 pieces, sequentially numbered on the reverse
- Multi parts construction & die stamped for ultimate fine detailing
- 7 enamel colours, electroplated in gold
- Avro Lancaster in metal relief & finished in antique silver creating hi/lo lights of contrasting details.
- Hand polished and enamelled by hand
- Fitted with jewellery style, non-turn, superior nickel clutch stud
- Personalised fitted presentation case with hand numbered Certificate of Authenticity
- Actual size 38 x 31.7mm

The Limited Edition Dambusters 617 Squadron 80th Anniversary 1943 -2023 Commemorative Badge is designed by and exclusively available from AWARD.

Code: LBDB *Dambusters 617 Squadron 80th Anniversary Commemorative Badge*

ONLY £49.95 Plus P&P

How to order

Order Online - www.awardmedals.com
Order by Phone - Call us between 9am to 5pm Monday to Friday on 01952 510053 Alternatively, please complete the order form enclosing a cheque/ postal order or completing the credit card details and send to:
Award Productions Ltd, PO Box 300, Shrewsbury, SY5 6WP, UK

Mr/Mrs/Miss/Ms ....
Address ....
.... Postcode ....
Daytime Tel. No. ....
Email address ....
I enclose my cheque/postal order for £ .... made payable to Award Productions Ltd or please debit my card account no: (Switch only)

Security Code: Last 3 digits on signature strip   Cards accepted: VISA MasterCard Maestro Solo Switch
Switch Issue No.
Expiry date: Valid from:
Signature ....
If cardholder's name, address and signature are different from the one shown, please include these details.

AWARD Order Form
PROUD TO SERVE

AWARD Productions Ltd, PO Box 300, Shrewsbury, SY5 6WP, UK
Please complete. Yes, please send me the following badge(s):

Code	Description	Price	Qty	Total £
LBDB	Dambusters 617 Squadron 80th Anniversary Badge	£49.95		
Delivery Subject to availability.		Postage/Packing/Insurance		£4.50
Please allow up to 28 days for delivery.			**Total £**	

AWARD Guarantee
The Dambusters 617 Squadron 80th Anniversary badge is brought to you by Award Productions Ltd, international medallist. You can order with complete confidence knowing that every item is backed by the AWARD guarantee. For full terms and conditions please visit our website: www.awardmedals.com

Award Productions Ltd, Registered in England No. 2001900, Shrewsbury SY4 4UG

SAL1

▼ For many years the Red Arrows used RAF Scampton as their base and primary UK training airfield. Looking out from this Hawk, the station's huge runway and some of its concrete V-Bomber dispersal areas are visible. **Cpl Graham Taylor/© UK MoD Crown Copyright 2023**

RAF Scampton
THE STATION

◀ The RAF Scampton station crest featured a bow and arrow. The bow represented the new route of the A15, the string followed Ermine Street and the arrow was the runway, as extended for the Vulcan. © **UK MoD Crown Copyright 2023**

Latterly home to the Royal Air Force Aerobatic Team The Red Arrows and No.1 Air Control Centre, RAF Scampton had a proud bomber heritage. Not only is it remembered as the station that launched the dams raid, but its personnel, including Wg Cdr Guy Gibson, won three Victoria Crosses

The airfield at Brattleby, close to the historic city of Lincoln, opened as a Royal Flying Corps (RFC) Home Defence Station in 1917. Tasked against the German Zeppelin airships, No.33 Squadron based its 'A' Flight at Air Station Brattleby and its Royal Aircraft Factory B.E.2, B.E.12 and F.E.2 biplanes were soon operational. As the Zeppelin menace waned, Brattleby turned to the preparation of aircrew and a variety of aircraft flew from the airfield with several different RFC and Royal Air Force training squadrons, until it closed in 1920, another victim of post-war disarmament.

And there the story might have ended, but in 1935 the RAF began a programme of expansion in response to the increasingly bellicose rumblings of Nazi Germany. Brattleby was one of several airfields reopened, while construction began on many more, a large number of them in Lincolnshire. Positioned more or less equally between the three villages of Aisthorpe, Brattleby and Scampton, the reborn facility, alongside the main A15 road heading north out of Lincoln, was no longer RAF Brattleby; now it was RAF Scampton.

Bomber Station
Through its wartime association with 617 Sqn and, perhaps, its Cold War nuclear role with the Avro Vulcan, Scampton is synonymous with bomber operations. In fact, even before 617 formed at the station in March 1943, Scampton had launched the RAF's first offensive action of World War II and continued to engage the enemy, while its aircrew had won the Victoria Cross on two occasions before 1940 was out.

Numbers IX(B) and 214 Squadrons were the first units into Scampton, arriving with their Handley Page Heyford and Vickers Virginia X biplane bombers in October 1936. Later to join 617 Sqn in destroying the *Tirpitz*, IX(B) Sqn remained at Scampton until March 1938, while 214 Sqn left in April 1937. Meanwhile, 148 Sqn came and went with its Hawker Audax and Vickers Wellesley aircraft, and Numbers 49 and 83 Squadrons arrived for a longer stay.

▲ Air Station Brattleby in 1917, with the A15 main road following the route of the Roman Ermine Street along the treeline in the background. **RAF Scampton Archive/© UK MoD Crown Copyright 2023**

In March 1938, No.49 Sqn brought its Hawker Hinds to Scampton from Worthy Down, Hampshire. Soon re-equipped with the Handley Page Hampden, the unit had a brief dalliance with the disastrous Avro Manchester in 1942, before converting onto the sublime Lancaster. The progression for 83 Sqn was similar, except that its Hinds arrived from Turnhouse, Midlothian.

Scampton launched the RAF's World War II offensive less than six hours after the declaration of war on September 3, 1939. Nine aircraft flew the mission, an offensive sweep off Wilhelmshaven, with Flying Officer Guy Gibson at the controls of one of six 83 Sqn Hampdens, while F/O Roderick 'Babe' Learoyd was among the pilots of 49 Sqn's three bombers. The raid achieved little other than to highlight just how unprepared Bomber Command was for operations.

Two VCs
Scampton continued to contribute bombers to the war effort, its crews doing their best with inadequate aircraft under difficult circumstances. On August 12, 1940, the Hampdens were in action against the Dortmund-Ems Canal and two of 83 Sqn's aircraft had already been shot down by intense anti-aircraft (AA) fire when Learoyd ran in to the target at low level. Caught in searchlights, his aircraft took two hits in one wing, but he remained calm at the controls and provided his bomb aimer with a stable platform for weapon release.

Learoyd nursed the Hampden back to England, arriving in the vicinity of Scampton at 2am. Although the aircraft was flyable, its hydraulic systems had been damaged and the wing flaps were inoperable. The undercarriage position indicators had also failed and rather than risk a crash landing in the dark, Learoyd circled for three hours, before making a safe landing at first light. He was awarded the Victoria Cross (VC) for his courage, skill and determination.

Remarkably, it was barely a month later that Scampton's second VC was won. Wireless operator/air gunner Sergeant John Hannah was just 18 years old when his 83 Sqn Hampden was hit on its second run against a target near Antwerp, on September 15. Under concentrated AA fire, his aircraft took a round in the bomb bay, leading to an explosion and serious fire. Both his own position and that of the rear gunner were immediately engulfed in fire and although the gunner had been forced to bail out, Hannah elected to remain »

▲ Several of Brattleby's training units used Sopwith Camels from 1918. B3801 was a 1F1 Camel converted as a two-seat trainer. RAF Scampton Archive/© UK MoD Crown Copyright 2023

at his post, fighting the fire with extinguishers and, when these expired, his logbook. He successfully prevented the fire from reaching ruptured fuel tanks in both wings, even as the aluminium floor beneath his feet melted and ammunition exploded all around.

Hannah, his face and eyes burned, then forced his way forwards. Discovering that the navigator had abandoned the Hampden, he passed the navigation logs and maps to the pilot and assisted him in navigating back to Scampton. Award of the Victoria Cross was, perhaps, inevitable.

New Bombers, New Squadron

Avro Manchesters began arriving at RAF Scampton in December 1941. By now the station had lost 150 Hampdens in combat, and the Manchester had entirely replaced it on No.83 Sqn by January 1942. Its crews were immediately dispirited with their new aircraft, as were those of 49 Sqn when it re-equipped, but delighted with the Lancasters that began arriving early in the summer.

▲ Personnel from No.49 Sqn gathered for this unit photograph in mid-1938, having arrived at Scampton earlier in the year. One of the squadron's Hind bombers forms the backdrop.

▼ This Wellesley served 148 Sqn. The unit formed at Scampton in June 1937, initially with six Audax biplanes and a single Wellesley. It moved on in March 1938. **both RAF Scampton Archive/© UK MoD Crown Copyright 2023**

Now 83 Sqn departed Scampton to become part of the Pathfinder Force at RAF Wyton, with 57 Sqn's Lancasters moving in. Spring 1943 saw 49 Sqn giving up its long association with Scampton as it flew out to make space for the formation of a new unit – 617 Sqn. Guy Gibson, now a Wing Commander with a Distinguished Flying Cross (DFC) from his service on 83 Sqn's Hampdens and fresh from command of 106 Sqn at nearby RAF Coningsby, returned to Scampton to form the squadron.

A little less than two months after its formation on March 21, 1943, No.617 Sqn despatched 19 Lancasters from Scampton's grass runways, bound for the great dams of the Ruhr. The raid and the squadron wrote history on the night of May 16/17, Gibson winning the station's third VC, but the time had come for the airfield to be modernised. The large four-engined Lancaster, weighed down by its impressive bomb load and enough fuel to reach deep into the Reich and back, was too heavy for operations from grass and, apart from training, Scampton closed for concrete runways to be laid.

New Runways, New Era

On October 20, 1944, Scampton launched seven 153 Sqn Lancasters on its return to operations. The Dambusters had long since

▶▲ John Hannah in apparently good spirits after his September 15, 1940, Victoria Cross sortie. The telegram is from Glasgow's Lord Provost. **both RAF Scampton Archive/© UK MoD Crown Copyright 2023**

left for RAF Coningsby and then Woodhall Spa, although 625 Sqn joined 153 Sqn for the final weeks of the war in Europe. Over winter 1945 and into spring 1946, Scampton once again housed 57 Sqn, this time as it converted from the Lancaster to Avro's successor, the Lincoln.

Number 100 Sqn was another brief resident, but the next front-line unit at Scampton was the US Air Force's 28th Bomb Wing (BW), which arrived with its Boeing B-29 Superfortress bombers in July 1948, in response to the crisis unfolding in Berlin. As the Soviet blockade of the German capital turned inexorably into the Berlin Airlift, the 301st BW replaced the 28th and remained until February 1949, when the RAF's 230 Operational Conversion Unit (OCU) began training Lincoln crews at the station.

The jet age arrived at Scampton in 1953, when 10, 18, 21 and 27 Squadrons all took up residence with their English Electric Canberras. They remained until 1955, when the base once again closed for rebuilding. Bomber Command was expanding its V-Force of nuclear bombers and Scampton was going to be a Vulcan station. Work began in earnest to build what remained the RAF's longest runway and one of its widest, sufficient to accommodate staggered Vulcan stream take-offs and long enough to require diversion of the A15 from its route along the ancient Roman road known as Ermine Street.

Dambusters Return

When RAF Scampton reopened in 1958, its first Vulcan unit was 617 Sqn, returning after a 15-year absence. This time it remained until December 1981, flying successive marks of Vulcan, armed with early free-fall nuclear weapons, the Avro Blue Steel missile and, ultimately, the WE.177 bomb. Numbers 83, 27 and 35 Squadrons successively joined 617 at what was now a major Vulcan base, 27 and 35 persisting on the type until March 1982.

With the drawdown of the Vulcan force, the Royal Air Force Aerobatic Team The Red Arrows took up residence at Scampton in 1983, remaining until 1996. The Central Flying School also made use of the station, operating between 1984 and 1995. When 'The Reds' departed for RAF Cranwell, no more than 20 miles (32km) away, in 1996, Scampton remained available only as their training location. The logic of basing RAFAT back at the station prevailed and in 2000 Scampton reopened. The Reds remained there until transitioning to RAF Waddington in 2022.

Although the Red Arrows fall under No.22 (Training) Group, RAF Scampton was latterly administered by No.1 Group. Apart from the Red Arrows, No.1 Air Control Centre [No.1 ACC] was Scampton's major resident. A 1 Group air defence radar unit, its permanent operations room, Control and Reporting Centre Scampton, provided resilience to the 24/7 coverage at RAF Boulmer. Training remained Scampton's primary responsibility, but it was also ready to maintain UK home defence coverage should there be a technical problem at Boulmer.

The unit's second responsibility was to provide deployable command and control »

▲ These 49 Sqn Hampdens were up from Scampton around mid-1939 for formation flying practice. The type was Scampton's primary equipment at the time.
◀ Flying Officer Roderick Learoyd, VC, shown in a formal portrait. **both RAF Scampton Archive/© UK MoD Crown Copyright 2023**

capability using containerised equipment that could be flown or driven anywhere worldwide to deliver very similar coverage to that of the permanent Control and Reporting Centres. Scampton was also home to the Mobile Meteorological Unit, staffed by full-time Reserve officers as part of the civilian Met Office.

Station Ethos and Heritage Centre

By the time of the Dambusters' 70th anniversary in 2013, RAF Scampton's days as a military flying station were numbered and it closed as an operational airfield on October 29, 2022. Its significance extended far beyond the Dambusters and Red Arrows, however, and it is likely to remain as an historic asset of national significance.

The Vulcan influence, especially the distinctive concrete dispersals typical of V-Bomber airfields, remains strong at Scampton, while many of its buildings, including all four Grade II listed C-Type hangars, are virtually unchanged since 1938. This leaves it as the best-preserved World War II bomber airfield in the UK; the practised eye will even spot the camouflage patterns, albeit faded, that were painted on the support buildings in wartime.

This heritage, combined with Scampton's Dambuster links, was the driving force behind the station's magnificent Ethos and Heritage Centre. Self-funded and staffed and maintained by volunteers, the centre existed primarily for the education of serving personnel, but was also available to other visitors by arrangement.

Located in the airfield's Number 2 hangar, which housed the Upkeep Lancasters in spring 1943, the centre included Wing Commander Gibson's office, restored to near original condition. It had a Dambusters room and so much more connected with RAF Scampton and wider RAF history. Among many gems, an obviously interim-standard woman's uniform from 1918 – featuring RAF and Royal Navy components – may well have been the very first uniform worn by a female member of the RAF; it was described as 'the holy grail of uniforms' by at least one expert.

Flying Future

Every significant anniversary stirs huge media and public interest in Scampton and the Dambusters. The dams raid is one of few individual missions that remain in the public psyche, and Scampton retains a proud association with the Dambusters.

▲ This student crew and instructors from No.230 OCU were preparaing for a Lincoln training sortie early in the 1950s.

▲▲ Surviving members of 617 Squadron assembled in front of a Lancaster for this photograph, taken just after the dams raid.

▶ Low passes are unlikely to be flown much lower than this one, in front of a Scampton hangar in June 1954. The Canberra belonged to No.27 Squadron.
all RAF Scampton Archive/© UK MoD Crown Copyright 2023

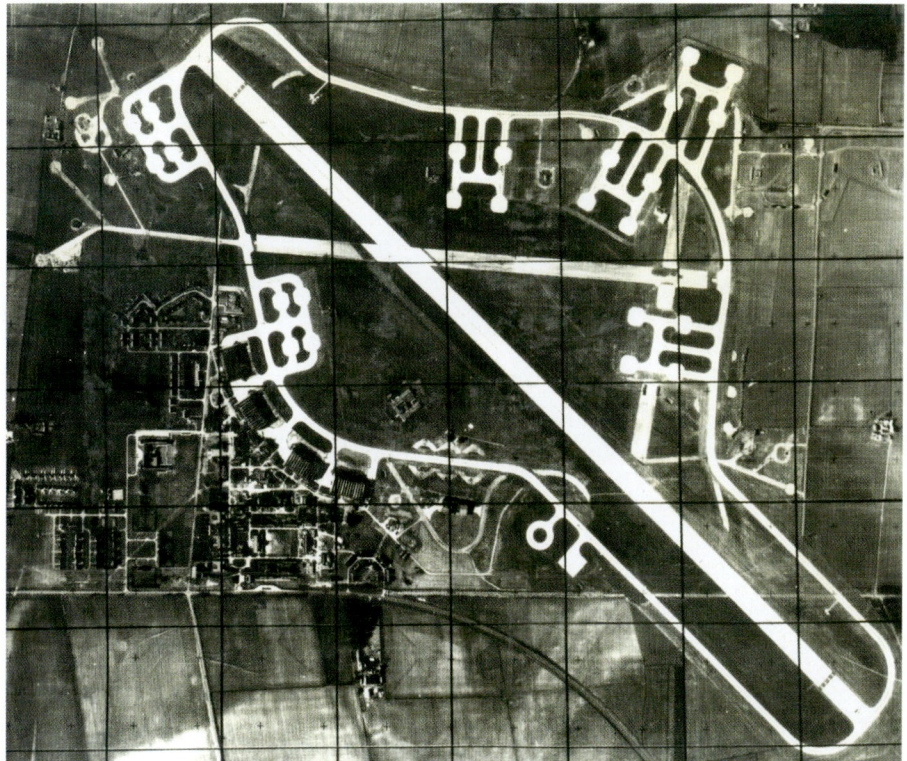

The RAF has perhaps also become embedded in the DNA of Lincolnshire, a region known as 'Bomber County'. Local people are proud of their association with the Service and the Dambusters, and there was understandably considerable concern when Scampton's closure was announced.

A 'Save Scampton' campaign attracted 6,500 signatures amidst fears the site would be redeveloped for housing or industrial use, its heritage and airfield status lost. Then, in February 2023, the local council announced that it was partnering with an investor to deliver a £300-million redevelopment that respected the site's iconic status.

Scampton Holdings intends to reactivate the station as an airfield while attracting commercial aviation and aerospace enterprises, heritage and tourism, and education and research activities.

Rolled out over a 15-year period, the plan will respect the airfield's protected status. Hangars 1 and 2 will be linked to create a museum, the linking structure creating a viewing platform; Scampton Holdings hopes the Red Arrows will continue to use the airspace above Scampton for training and practice, as they have since their move to Waddington.

Very much in the spirit of the station's former Ethos and Heritage Centre, Hangar 1 will tell the story of RAF Scampton including, of course, the Dambusters. Hangar 2, meanwhile, will be part workshop, part operational hub, with historic aircraft being restored under the watchful gaze of the public and flown from the nearby runway.

A Heritage Trail Tour will further reinforce the station's place in history as it takes visitors around elements of its World War II and Cold War infrastructure, including restored and repurposed buildings.

Other ideas for the ambitious scheme include the construction of a Red Arrows Visitor and VIP Experience Centre and the provision of a new location for the Museum of RAF Fire Fighting and its collection of appliances gathered over more than 100 years of RAF history. Scampton's future, it seems, is bright and its heritage will be remembered.

▲ RAF Scampton just before it reopened in 1958 for Vulcan operations. The dramatically long runway is obvious, with the diverted A15 sweeping off in a wide curve at the foot of the image.

▶ Blue Steel's volatile fuel required crews to wear protective suits for servicing. The complex weapon gained an interim operational capability with 617 Sqn on September 24, 1962. **both RAF Scampton Archive/© UK MoD Crown Copyright 2023**

▲ Scampton's Ethos and Heritage Centre included this Lancaster nose cone, modified with string and chinagraph pencil marks in the fashion of some of 617 Sqn's bomb aimers for the dams raid. **Flt Lt Sarah James**
▶ AOC 1 Group, AVM Stuart Atha, sits at Guy Gibson's desk in 2013, with Flt Lt Sarah James (third left), Scampton Station Commander Wg Cdr Richard Turner (third right) and volunteers and re-enactors. **via Flt Lt Sarah James**

THE RAID

Operation Chastise – Breaching the German Dams

On March 15, 1943 work began to form a new squadron for an operation against German dams. As **Robert Owen** details, the operation would take place during the third or fourth week of May and place itself prominently in the chronicles of military history

▼ Flt Lt Maltby's Upkeep breaches the Möhne dam, as Flt Lt Martin provides support. The powerhouse on the dam's airside burns fiercely after being hit by Flt Lt Hopgood's misguided weapon. **Mark Postlethwaite**

Air Chief Marshal Harris chose Wing Commander Guy Gibson, then commanding officer of No.106 Sqn, to lead the unit that was to attack the dams. He had known Gibson for a long time and held him in high regard as a determined and enthusiastic pilot who led from the front. He was the ideal choice for this difficult and demanding operation.

Twenty-one crews were selected from No.5 Group squadrons. Contrary to popular belief they were not all recipients of medals, nor had they all completed at least one tour of operations and neither were they all personally known to Gibson. Nevertheless, regardless of experience, all had demonstrated determination and high qualities of airmanship – a 'press on' spirit. Secrecy was paramount, so much so that for the first week even Gibson had no idea of the nature of his target. All he knew was that he was to train his crews to fly low at night, and release a bomb at 100ft (30m) and 240mph (386km/h). He was told: "It will be convenient to practise this over water."

On March 25, the crews began to gather at Scampton, north of Lincoln. At first the new squadron had to beg, borrow or steal equipment. The aircraft to carry Upkeep would not arrive until the third week of April, so the aircrews began to practise using standard aircraft on loan from other units.

Navigation on this operation would be paramount. Crews were sent off on long daylight cross-countries, flying at 2,000ft (610m) to begin with, reducing to 500ft (152m) and then 150ft (46m) as skill and confidence grew. Bomb aimers 'eyeballed' the route, using roller maps and picking up visual landmarks, which they relayed back to the navigator sitting back inside the aircraft.

They flew singly at first, and then in small formations. Inevitably, some returned with foliage attached to their aircraft, or with trailing aerials pulled out after snagging on a ground obstruction. Despite this there were no serious accidents and soon the crews were becoming proficient. The operation was to be carried out in moonlight, but with only one full moon period until its launch there would be few moonlight nights on which to practise.

To overcome this, four Lancasters were fitted with a synthetic night flying system, the pilot wearing coloured goggles, while the cockpit Perspex was tinted a complementary colour, creating the impression of moonlight while flying by day. Other crewmembers, not so equipped, could act as 'check pilots', looking out for obstructions to reduce the risk of nasty surprises.

Insects squashed against the Perspex posed another problem – they could easily be mistaken for approaching obstructions. Pilots learned to distinguish between these and real obstacles by moving their head from side to side. Distant objects stayed still – the flies appeared to move.

Bombing Solutions

As navigation improved, attention turned to bombing. Height and speed were critical factors, and the weapon would have to be released at a given distance from the target. The standard low-level bombsight was not accurate enough.

An ingenious, but simple solution was found. The main targets had two towers on their crest, the distance between them being measured from aerial photographs. A simple triangulation sight was devised with a peephole at one angle and two nails as sighting marks on the others. Holding the peephole to his eye, the bomb aimer observed the approaching target. When the towers on the target coincided with the nails, the bomb was released.

Bomb aimers made their own variations, some using chinagraph or tape marks on the nose Perspex, with a length of taught string to obtain the correct angle of sight. Screens representing the towers were erected on the bombing range at Wainfleet, and soon crews were achieving the accuracy desired.

The determination of the exact height for Upkeep's release was more problematic. It had been hoped that practice might make perfect, but at dusk or night it was almost impossible. The standard altimeter was not sensitive enough at low level and barometric pressures over the target would be unpredictable. Radio altimeters could not be relied upon in the hills surrounding reservoirs.

Various methods were suggested, including a wire with a weight (some joked, the navigator) trailed beneath the aircraft, indication of the correct height being given by the jolt as it hit the water. None was satisfactory. Scientists at Farnborough eventually resurrected an idea dating from World War I. A spotlight was fitted beneath the nose of the aircraft, with another under the belly, their beams angled downwards to intersect at the required height below the aircraft.

As the Lancaster descended the lights would come together to make the figure '8' on the surface of the water, indicating that the aircraft was at the correct height. The navigator watched them from the cockpit blister and issued 'up/down' instructions to the pilot over the intercom. The lights were shielded as much as possible, nevertheless it was rather unnerving to think about flying in to attack an as yet unknown and presumably defended target, lit up for the enemy gunners to see.

It was a simple idea and with little practice pilots found that they could fly accurately to within a few feet of the original specified height of 150ft. Towards the end of April, after the failure of the weapon during trials from this height, the lights were adjusted to converge at just 60ft (18m), a frighteningly low height for a heavy aircraft, with a wing span of 102ft (31m).

Training in Earnest

By mid-April the first of the specially modified aircraft were beginning to arrive for allocation to crews. By the end of the month it was time » to co-ordinate the various elements into an operational plan. It was intended that Wg Cdr Gibson would control the main attacks over the target by direct voice communication, calling in each aircraft in turn. The Lancaster's standard fit was not suitable for this and each of the modified aircraft would be fitted with a VHF radio for this purpose. Radios and workbenches were set up in the squadron offices in order to permit the practice and evolution of signals technique.

Training was progressing well by day and night. Three night routes were devised to represent, as far as possible, the nature of those being planned for the operation. In addition to the Howden and Derwent dams north west of Sheffield, two other reservoirs, Eyebrook, near Uppingham and Abberton at Colchester, were selected as 'targets', with dummy towers erected on the dam at Eyebrook to provide an aiming point for bomb aimers, although no bombs would be dropped at any of these locations.

From May 11, selected squadron pilots were given the opportunity to drop an inert Upkeep at Reculver. Flying in at right angles to the coast, they released their weapons to come ashore, some bouncing over the earth embankment to land in the oyster beds beyond. Unable to use the spotlights in daylight, a number of pilots released their weapon from below 60ft, their aircraft suffering damage from the plume thrown up by Upkeep's initial impact with the sea, demonstrating yet another hazard of this method of attack.

While the squadron trained and Barnes Wallis perfected Upkeep, reconnaissance Spitfires were flying high over the dams, bringing back photographs to enable interpreters to monitor the reservoir levels and the state of the defences. The attack would be mounted when the water level was at its highest, and during the period of the May full moon, not later than May 19.

Only the Möhne dam was defended, with twin torpedo nets strung across the lake to protect the wall and three 20mm flak guns – one on top of each of the towers, and another on the north east end of the parapet. There was a group of three more light flak guns in the fields below the dam.

However, there was one feature that caused the interpreters some concern. A number of short blocks were appearing, spaced out along the parapet and they were not immediately identifiable. Might they be further defences? The truth was less alarming – they were dummy fir trees, intended as a measure to conceal the dam from low-level attack. As far as can be ascertained, the timing of their arrival was nothing more than coincidence. The other dams appeared undefended, but the topography around these created a more difficult run in and climb out after bombing, making them far from easy targets.

By the end of the second week of May, Upkeep had been perfected; the aircraft had been delivered and crews could fly, navigate and bomb from low level. The latter elements were brought together in a series of exercises conducted during the two nights of May 13 and 14. Either in small formations, or flying individually, aircraft flew short cross countries and made 'attacks' on Eyebrook and Abberton reservoirs, with other crews making spotlight runs at Derwent Valley, over the Wash and off the Yorkshire coast. The first night revealed a number of shortcomings in tactics and control, but these were swiftly ironed out, and the second exercise proved all was ready.

Preparing for Action
During the afternoon of May 15, Wallis flew to Scampton, ready to supervise final adjustments to the aircraft mechanism and observe the loading of the live Upkeeps.

Transformer Station | Engine House

◀ The Eder dam pre-war.

◀▼ Gibson's Lancaster with Upkeep attached.

▼ The Möhne in an aerial reconnaissance photograph prior to the raid. **all RAF (AHB)/© UK MoD Crown Copyright 2023**

Gibson attended a final planning conference at No.5 Group Headquarters at Grantham, before returning to Scampton, where he and Wallis briefed the two Flight Commanders and Section Leaders on the outline operational plan.

On leaving the meeting Gibson received news that his dog, whose name he had chosen to confirm the breaching of the Möhne dam, had been run over and killed outside the camp. It might have seemed an omen, but Gibson had little time to brood as he concentrated on last-minute preparations.

The morning of May 16 dawned bright and sunny. The met forecast for that night was favourable for the operation. While groundcrew checked, armed and fuelled the aircraft, aircrew were summoned to briefing sessions. Individual crew trades were given specialist briefings by their Section Leaders during the morning. No.5 Group's Signals Leader, who would be receiving their messages that night, issued the wireless operators with a new system of code words. The navigators were provided with the route details and then went off to prepare their flight plans.

Work continued through the day until mid-afternoon, when the tannoy ordered all 617 Squadron aircrew to Scampton's main briefing room. Service police checked their identities as they entered. When all were present, Gibson entered the room to brief his crews on Operation Chastise, accompanied by Air Vice-Marshal Cochrane, Wallis and the Station Commander. Clearly this was no normal briefing. »

Operational Plan

After Gibson had confirmed the targets, he proceeded to outline the operational plan. Nineteen aircraft would be detailed. The first wave would consist of three sections, each of three aircraft, taking off with ten minutes between sections. They were to take a route that overflew East Anglia to Southwold, crossed the North Sea and entered Holland at the Scheldt Estuary.

East of Eindhoven they would head north east to Rees on the River Rhine, before heading east to skirt north of the Ruhr then turn south west to the Möhne dam, which they would attack first. Any aircraft still with its bomb after this was breached was then to go on to attack the Eder dam. After a successful attack on this objective, any remaining aircraft that had not bombed would go on to the Sorpe dam.

A second wave of five aircraft, each flying independently, would head out across north Lincolnshire and the North Sea. Passing between the Frisian Islands they would cross the Dutch coast coincident with the first wave and head north east over the Zuider Zee, joining the southern route just east of Rees, following it as far as the area of the Möhne, but continuing on to the nearby Sorpe.

A third wave of five aircraft, again flying independently, would take off some two hours after the first wave and form an airborne reserve that would be directed to whichever of the three main targets remained after the earlier attacks. Should all three have been successfully breached, No.5 Group HQ would instruct the reserve aircraft by radio to attack smaller dams in the Ruhr area.

The entire flight to and from the targets would be made at low level. Aircraft could briefly climb to 500ft, but only if essential to identify approaching turning points, since this might expose them to light flak. The routes had been planned to avoid known flak as far as possible, but not all was known. If they kept low they would be gone before any flak could draw a bead

▲ Gibson, to the right, holding a pipe, with his dog and squadron members. RAF Scampton Archive/© UK MoD Crown Copyright 2023

▲▲ Photographed on May 26, 1943, Gibson snatches a few moments to relax.

▲▶ AVM Cochrane did much of the operational planning for the raid. both RAF (AHB)/© UK MoD Crown Copyright 2023

▲ Gibson flew Lancaster Type 464 (Provisioning) ED932/AJ-G on May 16/17, 1943. **Pete West**

on them. If Gibson was shot down, or had to abort, Flt Lt John Hopgood would lead the attack on the Möhne, and Sqn Ldr Henry 'Dinghy' Young that on the Eder.

Attacks on the Möhne and Eder were to be made across the lake, at right angles to the dam. Aircraft were to start spinning their bombs 10 minutes before they made their run. The attacks would be co-ordinated by Gibson, who would call each aircraft in in turn, using the VHF radio. Attacks were to be made at 60ft and 220mph (354km/h), and at least three minutes was to be allowed between each attack.

The attacks on the Sorpe were to adopt a different technique. Because this was an earthen dam – a concrete core buttressed by long, sloping banks of earth and not suited to Upkeep (which had been developed to attack concrete gravity dams) – aircraft were to make their run across the lake, parallel to the dam wall and release their Upkeep at its mid-point from as low as possible and at 180 mph (290km/h). Upkeep was not to be spun – in effect being used as a large depth charge.

The Möhne

Because of their longer route to the Dutch coast the second wave took off first, headed by Flt Lt Robert Barlow at 21:28. Flt Lt Joe McCarthy experienced a coolant leak at start up and had to transfer to the reserve aircraft.

Gibson led his formation away 11 minutes later, followed by the formations of Sqn Ldrs Young and Maudslay. After crossing the Dutch coast slightly off track, Gibson's formation headed low across Holland and on to the Rhine, encountering minimal opposition. Passing into Germany they ran into unexpected flak near Dulmen, the position of which was radioed back in order to warn following aircraft, and at this point it is believed that Hopgood's aircraft was hit, injuring several crew and causing damage to the Lancaster. Displaying the qualities for which the crews had been selected, he continued on to the Möhne.

The two following formations also encountered spasmodic flak on this leg, but escaped injury. Flying at tree-top height south of Borken, Flt Lt William Astell's aircraft struck a pylon and crashed, killing all on board.

The remaining eight aircraft pressed on to the Möhne.

Approaching half past midnight and in the face of fierce opposition, Gibson made the first attack. His Upkeep bounced three times, sank and exploded, sending a gigantic plume into the air and over the dam. At first it was thought that the dam had gone, but as the water subsided it was seen to be intact.

Hopgood made the next run, but without the element of surprise his aircraft was hit and set on fire. His bomb was released fractionally late and bounced over the dam, destroying the powerhouse beyond. Struggling for height, Hopgood turned away from the valley. By a miracle, two of his crew managed to get out before the aircraft exploded at 500ft.

Flt Lt Harold Martin was next to attack. Gibson flew in alongside with his lights on to distract the German gunners. The technique was partially successful, but at the moment of release Martin felt a jolt as flak hit his starboard wing, fortunately causing only minor damage. Martin's Upkeep struck the water, but veered off to explode by the »

▼ The building housing Scampton's main briefing room is shown here in the early post-war years. It remains largely unchanged. **RAF Scampton Archive/© UK MoD Crown Copyright 2023**

▲ Flying Officer Astell before promotion to Flight Lieutenant.

▲▲ Group Captain Whitworth, station commander.

▲▶ Flt Lt Harold 'Micky' Martin and crewmembers on the roof of the Air Ministry in London, after receiving awards for their part in Operation Chastise. all RAF (AHB)/© UK MoD Crown Copyright 2023

lake's southern shore, in doing so putting out of action the gun on the left hand tower.

Next to attack was Sqn Ldr Young. Martin flew in alongside, while Gibson flew airside of the dam, engaging the flak. Young's weapon seemed a perfect shot, but still the dam appeared intact.

As the fifth aircraft made its run, its pilot, Flt Lt David Maltby, thought he saw the crest begin to crumble, and nudged his aircraft slightly to port. Again it was a perfect shot. As the plume subsided from its detonation Martin, flying beyond the dam, saw the wall roll over and a torrent burst through, surging over the remains of the powerhouse as 130 million tons of water began to inundate the valley.

The Eder

After broadcasting the codeword confirming a successful attack on the Möhne at 00:56, Gibson ordered Young and the remaining three aircraft still with their Upkeeps to proceed with him to the Eder dam. On reaching the target area, the crews found the valleys filling with mist, making identification of the reservoir difficult. Gibson found the target and fired a red Very light above it to summon the others.

There were no defences, but the hills surrounding the Eder were higher and steeper than those at the Möhne. The serpentine shape of the reservoir precluded a long straight run to the target; instead aircraft had to dive down to the lake following a side valley, aiming for a spit of land. On reaching the spit they had to turn sharply to port, level out at 60ft and make sure they were not travelling too fast to make their attack. Immediately after release full power had to be applied to enable them to make a climbing turn to starboard, following the valley and avoiding a steep hillside rising beyond the dam.

Sqn Ldr Maudslay and Flt Lt David Shannon made a number of individual attempts, trying for the correct approach. Eventually Shannon released his Upkeep. It bounced twice and struck the dam, which remained intact.

Maudslay tried again, and again, eventually releasing his weapon too late. It struck the parapet, detonating just behind the Lancaster, which was seen banking steeply in the flash of the explosion. Gibson called Maudslay, who was heard to reply very faintly. Nothing more

◀ Flight Lieutenant Joe McCarthy attacked the Sorpe. Here he talks to King George VI during his May 27 visit to RAF Scampton.

▼ Dated August 21, 1943, this chart shows the planned routes and actual routes followed on May 16/17. The letters refer to individual aircraft codes. **both RAF (AHB)/© UK MoD Crown Copyright 2023**

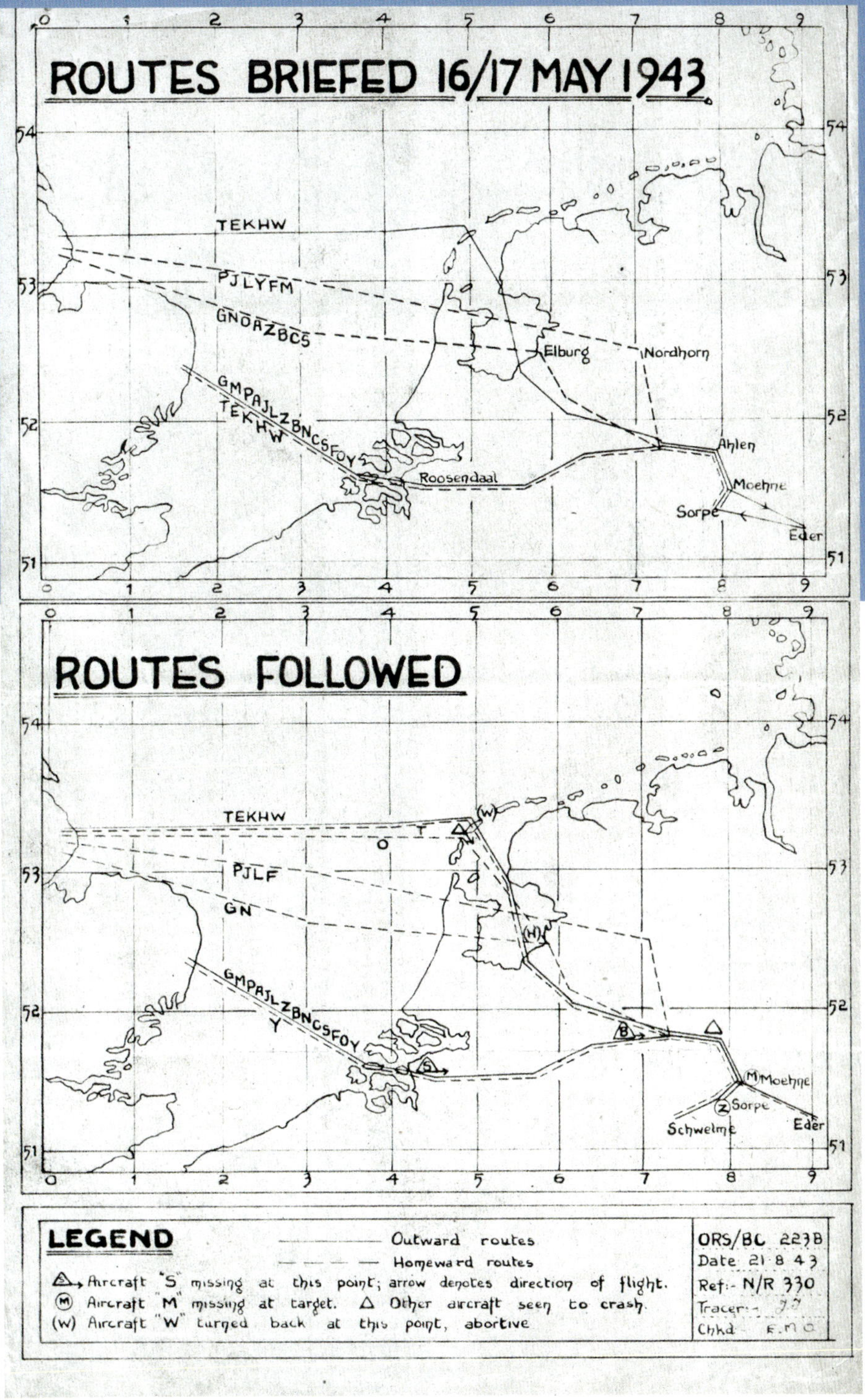

was heard from him, leading to contemporary supposition that his aircraft had been destroyed by the blast. In fact Maudslay was heading for home, only to be shot down by light flak as he neared Emmerich, on the Rhine, with the loss of all on board.

This left only the Upkeep carried by P/O Knight. After several attempts, Knight made a successful release. His Upkeep bounced three times, struck the dam and exploded. As his aircraft climbed away, the navigator, looking back through the astrodome, saw a hole punched through the wall, leaving the parapet as a momentary bridge, before it too crumbled into the maelstrom as 202 million tons of water were released.

Their job done and with the codeword 'Dinghy' confirming their success sent at 01:54, the Lancasters set course for base, heading back to the Möhne, before skirting north of the Ruhr and taking three differing routes to avoid the defences.

Young was unlucky. As he crossed the coast of Holland his aircraft was hit by a final burst of fire from the ground defences and came down in the sea. There were no survivors. »

The Sorpe

The aircraft detailed to attack the Sorpe dam met with little success. Crossing the Frisian Islands, Flt Lt Les Munro's Lancaster was hit by a single round of light flak that took out the intercom. Without it the crew could only communicate by written messages, rendering impossible the co-ordination required for a successful attack. Reluctantly, Munro turned for home with his weapon.

Pilot Officer Vernon Byers was shot down, again by a chance shot from a battery on Texel, crashing into the Waddenzee with total loss of life – the operation's first casualty.

P/O Geoff Rice misjudged his height over the Zuider Zee, striking the water. He managed to hold the Lancaster, but the Upkeep had been torn from the bomb bay. With water pouring out of the rear of the aircraft, Rice too was forced to abort and head for home.

Flt Lt Barlow crossed into Holland and headed for the Rhine. As he turned east at Rees, his aircraft collided with high-tension cables and crashed in flames. Its Upkeep rolled from the wreckage. The self-destruct pistol intended to destroy the weapon in such an eventuality failed to function, presenting the Germans with an intact example of this unique weapon.

This left only Flt Lt McCarthy of those detailed to attack the Sorpe. He was successful in reaching his target, where there were no defences, but mist was beginning to form. After several attempts he successfully released his weapon, which detonated in the water near the crest, but the dam remained intact. Unable to do anything more, he turned for home, hoping that others might come and repeat the attack with greater success.

This left only the five aircraft of the airborne reserve. They crossed into Holland, following the southern route flown by the formations of Gibson, Young and Maudslay.

▲ Flight Sergeant Ken Brown, a Canadian pilot, flew as part of the third wave.

◀▲ Flight Lieutenant David Maltby relates his experiences at the Möhne to the King.

▲▶ Flight Lieutenant David John Shannon attacked the Eder.

◀ Flight Lieutenant Les Munro and fellow New Zealander, Flying Officer Leonard Chambers (left), both flew on the raid. Chambers was 'Micky' Martin's wireless operator.

▶ Water pours through the breached Möhne dam in a German photograph above, which also shows the ineffectual fake fir trees designed to camouflage its crest. The reconnaissance photograph below was taken on May 17, 1943. **RAF Scampton Archive/© UK MoD Crown Copyright 2023 and RAF (AHB)/© UK MoD Crown Copyright 2023**

◀ Pilot Officer Knight talks with Gibson and the King.
all RAF (AHB)/© UK MoD Crown Copyright 2023

Pilot Officer Lewis Burpee approached the German night fighter base at Gilze Rijen, east of Tilburg, along his route. Witness accounts vary, but he was either hit by light flak, or dazzled by a searchlight that caught the aircraft full in its beam. Out of control, the Lancaster crashed into an airfield building and exploded. Almost as the aircraft crashed, a message was sent from Group re-assigning it to the Sorpe, but its receipt was never acknowledged.

Pilot Officer Warner Ottley was approaching the German town of Hamm when his crew received the message from No.5 Group HQ that they should attack the Lister dam. Almost immediately light flak opened up on the aircraft, setting the starboard inner engine on fire. The Lancaster rapidly became uncontrollable and crashed into woodland, where it exploded. By a miracle, Sgt Frank Tees, the rear gunner, survived, bruised and burned, when the tail section broke away on impact, with him still in his turret. The remaining crew were not so lucky.

Flt Sgt Kenneth Brown made his way to the Sorpe dam as instructed. Like McCarthy, he found thickening mist filling the valley and had difficulties finding the correct approach. On his sixth run, after dropping incendiaries to provide a datum, he finally released his Upkeep, which also exploded close to its intended target. As with McCarthy, no breach was observed. Returning over Holland, Brown's aircraft was fired upon as it approached the Helder, the flak severely damaging the fuselage while the crew ducked down inside. Then they were through and out over the North Sea, heading for Scampton and safety.

The Ennepe
Pilot Officer William Townsend was diverted to the Ennepe dam. En route his Lancaster came under concentrated »

▶ Photo-reconnaissance Spitfires provided vivid evidence of the devastation downstream of the Möhne. The town of Boesperde (below) was imaged on May 17, while a damaged railway viaduct near Heidecke is shown at right. **both RAF (AHB)/© UK MoD Crown Copyright 2023**

fire from light flak batteries and as a phalanx of shells headed for him, he spotted woodland ahead. Pushing down the Lancaster's nose, Townsend flew along a firebreak while his crew saw the tracer scything through the treetops as the enemy gunners sought to follow the Lancaster's progress. They escaped unscathed and reached their target area, encountering mist-filled valleys. Finding a reservoir and dam, identified as the Ennepe, they made their attack.

Their Upkeep bounced across the lake, but sank short of the dam. As the water plume subsided, the wall was still intact. They headed for home, the last crew of Operation Chastise to make an attack. Dawn was breaking as they crossed Holland, and they diverted from the planned route in an attempt to slip out unnoticed.

As they approached Texel a heavy gun opened fire, some of its shells bouncing off the water and over the Lancaster, so low were they flying. Turning away, Townsend sought a less defended track along which to make his final exit. He was successful and landed at Scampton at 06:15, the last of the survivors to return. Subsequent assessment and examination of German records post-war suggests that he and his crew had, in fact, attacked the Bever dam.

The final crew, led by Flt Lt Cyril Anderson, also experienced navigational difficulties. Detailed to attack the Dieml dam, outbound the crew had run into flak around Dulmen, and were forced off course by searchlights. Suffering problems with their guns and unable to establish their position, the crew decided to abandon the mission and return along the southern route. Returning safely, they incurred Gibson's displeasure later that morning, followed by an ignominious posting back to their previous squadron.

Back to Scampton
Wallis, Harris and Cochrane, who had returned to Scampton from No.5 Group HQ at Grantham, where they had been monitoring the operation's progress, met the returning crews. The atmosphere was a cocktail of jubilation and sorrow. Two of the three primary targets had been destroyed, but eight of the specially modified Lancasters had been lost. Of the 133 aircrew that set ›››

▼ Another German photograph shows water cascading through the Eder. **RAF (AHB)/© UK MoD Crown Copyright 2023**

Avro Type 464 (Provisioning) Lancaster

Twenty-two Lancaster B.Mk III aircraft were converted to carry the spinning Upkeep mines although in the event, only 19 took part in the dams raid. Under the designation Type 464 (Provisioning), several adjustments were made to enable them to carry and deliver the unique 9,250lb weapon.

The Lancasters' bomb doors were removed and the 'bouncing bombs' were attached to the underside of the aircraft between two V-shaped callipers mounted either side of the fuselage. The mines were rotated at 500rpm by a belt linked to a hydraulic motor usually used in submarines to power their control surfaces. The standard mid-upper turret was removed and its aperture faired over to save weight and drag.

The 60ft release height required to ensure that Upkeep skipped across the water was impossible to judge accurately with the Lancaster's altimeter. Engineers at Farnborough therefore devised a method of accurately determining the bomber's height by attaching two modified Aldis spot lamps, mounted underneath the aircraft at an angle, to make their respective beams merge when the Lancaster was 60ft above the water's surface.

The forward lamp was fitted underneath the nose, in the location normally occupied by the bomb-aimer's camera, while the other was located centrally on the sloping fairing behind the Upkeep mine. They were aimed to shine to the right-hand side of the aircraft, enabling the navigator to see their beams as he looked out of the blister on the right-hand side of the cockpit.

The Lancaster's standard bombsight could not be used for such a low-level attack and, ultimately, three potential, but very makeshift alternatives were developed. All owed their design to the laws of geometry and triangulation. First was the handheld wooden Dann sight, named after its inventor and made famous in *The Dam Busters* movie of 1955. However, it was thought to be so difficult to use accurately in flight that all but two of the crews tasked with attacking the Möhne and Eder dams chose to use either a piece of string attached to either side of the bomb-aimer's nose blister, or two chinagraph lines drawn on the blister itself, to determine – by triangulation – their distance from the target and, therefore, the moment to release the mine.

Another simple adjustment believed unique to dams raid aircraft was the provision of 'stirrups' to prevent the front gunner's feet from dangling in front of the bomb aimer during the attack.

Tom Allett

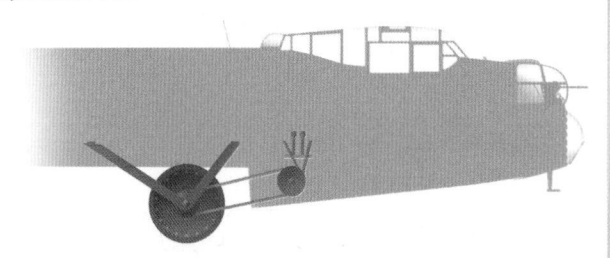

▼ Diagram showing the arrangement of the calliper arms and hydraulic motor.

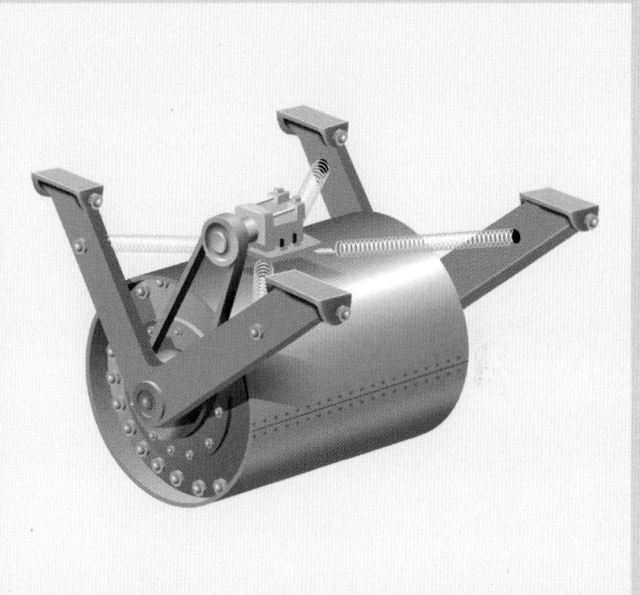

▲ The motor and its belt drive are shown here. The coiled lines below approximate to the system used to hold the arms against the Upkeep. A standard bomb slip (or release mechanism) held the lines taught until bomb release, when they relaxed to open the arms. No firm evidence of this arrangement survives. **both Pete West**

▼ Gibson's aircraft, showing the Upkeep modifications. **RAF (AHB)/© UK MoD Crown Copyright 2023**

▲ Spitfire PRXI photo-reconnaissance aircraft flew pre- and post-raid missions to gather data on the targets and provide bomb damage assessment. **RAF (AHB)/© UK MoD Crown Copyright 2023**

out, 56 had failed to return, only three of whom would survive as prisoners of war.

Harris, who had been dismissive of the operation, now told Wallis: "You could sell me a pink elephant," but that was of little comfort to the engineer, distraught at the losses, despite Gibson's reassurance that they were not his fault. Of those who returned, 34 would receive medals commemorating their skill, courage and determination, including the highest honour, the Victoria Cross, for their leader.

In Germany, as dawn broke the full impact of the raid became apparent. The floods thundering down the Möhne and Eder valleys had swept away all in their path. Roads, railways and bridges had been obliterated by the force of the water, travelling in the region of 40mph (64km/h), with an initial wave some 35ft (10.7m) high.

The water from the Möhne eventually reached as far as Duisburg, that from the Eder inundating parts of the industrial district of Kassel, flooding acres of valuable agricultural land, eroding fertile topsoil and drowning significant numbers of livestock. Inevitably there was high human cost, 1,294 people lost their lives, many of them foreign workers from a camp in the Möhne valley.

Industrial output was significantly affected. Although only the destroyed factories were recorded, production at many more was significantly reduced. The water wrecked electrical equipment, while mud and silt got into bearings and machinery, including that of the pumping stations, vital to the Ruhr's water supply. There was no water for industrial processes, or domestic supply – for drinking and washing. Electrical generation and distribution were severely disrupted.

In order to resume production, tools and equipment were brought from factories elsewhere in Germany – robbing Peter to pay Paul. Even when production was resumed, dislocation of the transport system meant shortages of raw materials, and finished products could not be despatched to where they were needed. The great clear-up caused the redeployment of workers, machinery and materials from other vital war tasks. Priority was given to rebuilding the dams, personnel being taken from construction of the Atlantic Wall defences to do the work.

The Möhne dam had been repaired by September and the Eder by the following month, sufficient to collect the winter rains, but not until several years following the war would either be permitted to contain their full volume. In case of further attacks, men, weapons, barrage balloons and smoke screens were committed to defend other dams throughout Germany. There they would sit and wait in vain, for attacks that never came.

Capitalising on Success

Photographic reconnaissance Spitfires flew high overhead, collecting imagery for interpreters keen to assess the full effects of the operation. Every opportunity was taken to capitalise on its success. Winston Churchill, in America at the time, marshalled it in support of his argument to persuade the Americans to maintain focus on the European war, rather than the Pacific.

Leaflets showing the breached Möhne dam were dropped to boost the morale of those in German-occupied territories. Not surprisingly, in Germany restrictions were imposed on letters and news from the affected areas in a futile attempt to play down the scale of the damage.

Post-war attempts to label the dams raid an expensive sideshow, on the basis that Ruhr industry was not significantly affected, do the operation a disservice. Comparison of the actual results of Chastise to (often exaggerated) propaganda reports of the destruction is unjust. The raid was an integral part of the Battle of the Ruhr – Bomber Command's ongoing offensive at the time. The planners had identified that the cumulative effect of breaching both the Möhne and the Sorpe dams would be greater than the destruction of one alone, but the different nature of construction mitigated the likelihood of this being achieved.

The facts remain. In one operation, 19 aircraft had caused more damage over a wider area than had 596 aircraft during a single attack on Dortmund eleven nights earlier. However, the legacy extended far beyond the material damage caused that night. A small force had demonstrated that it could navigate deep into Germany's industrial heartland, locate a small target thought to be impervious to aerial bombardment, and destroy it with a precision attack, causing a disproportionate amount of damage.

The decision to breach the dams had resulted in the creation of a specialist unit, whose further precision bombing exploits, often utilising other weapons generated by the innovative mind of Barnes Wallis, would conclusively demonstrate the value of accurately targeted air power, effectively delivered, by a small, highly trained and determined force.

▲ All those who took part in the dams raid were listed on a board fixed to the wall in Gibson's restored office at RAF Scampton. **Flt Lt Sarah James**

more than just **modelling**

The excitement is building

Airfix.com

▲ The exact relationship of this photograph to Urquhart is unknown. It was dedicated to his memory by 'Johnny' Johnson and may show Maudslay dropping an Upkeep at Reculver. *via* Simon Muggleton

THE COMMONWEALTH CONNECTION

Flying Officer Robert Alexander Urquhart, DFC

Airmen from Australia, Canada and New Zealand were among the dams raid crews. **Simon Muggleton** tells the story of one of them

Robert Alexander Urquhart was one of many Commonwealth airmen in the RAF. His short flying career ended as navigator on Lancaster 'AJ-Z', flown by Squadron Leader Maudslay, DFC, on No.617 Sqn's May 15/16, 1943, mission. Their badly damaged Lancaster was easy prey for German defences as it limped towards home after the attack and it was shot down just inside Germany. The crew perished; Urquhart was just two months short of his 24th birthday.

Robert Urquhart was born on August 2, 1919 at Moose Jaw, Saskatchewan, Canada, to Susie Grace and Alexander James Urquhart. His father worked as an accountant with the Canadian Pacific Railway. He had a brother and two sisters, and enjoyed a thorough education, with many sporting activities including baseball, rugby, hockey and various track events. He also became proficient in first aid and photography.

By 1937 Robert had completed a drafting course and took a six-month job as a callboy for crews on the Canadian Pacific Railway. Leaving this temporary position, he embarked on a new career, enrolling on a course of jewellery engraving. This lasted two years, before he changed careers again, moving to Vancouver, British Columbia to become the stock manager/buyer for The Aristocratic Hamburger Company.

Answering the Call

By now Holland and Belgium had been overrun, and it was the turn of France to face the German onslaught. Great Britain was being threatened and it called upon the citizens of the Commonwealth and its Dominions to help in the fight. Robert Urquhart applied to join the Royal Canadian Air Force (RCAF) by letter, on May 21, 1940.

He was quick to complete his attestation papers, at the RCAF Recruiting Center in Vancouver on June 19. He was obviously

▲ On July 20, 1945, the *London Gazette* announced that F/O Urquhart had been awarded the DFC, 'with effect from 15 May 1943'. *via* Simon Muggleton

keen to get into uniform, because he then volunteered to enrol as a private with the 2nd Battalion Canadian Seaforth Regiment, under the Non-Permanent Active Militia, while waiting for a response from the RCAF.

Urquhart learned that the RCAF had accepted him to train as a pilot/observer after only a month with the Seaforths. He signed up on January 9, 1941 with the rank of Aircraftman 2, and was posted to No.2 Manning Depot at Brandon, Manitoba. He quickly acquired a nickname, 'Turk', which remained with him throughout his career.

RCAF training began on April 10, 1941 and Sergeant Urquhart passed out on January 5, 1942, with a final mark of 72.2% and total night and day flying time of 140 hours. He was promoted Pilot Officer the same day and sent to the RCAF Depot at Halifax on January 7, to await posting. Two months later he arrived in the UK, enrolling with No.2 (Air Observers) Advanced Flying Unit at Cumberland, on April 24, 1942.

On May 19, P/O Urquhart was posted to No.14 Operational Training Unit at Cottesmore, Rutland, flying Ansons and Hampdens as first navigator and bomb aimer. He flew with American pilot P/O Joe McCarthy on August 11, 1942, both men later taking part in the dams raid.

After two months of training, Urquhart flew his first operation ('op'), as a Hampden navigator, to Dusseldorf, on July 31. He flew the four-hour sortie as one of 630 aircraft taking part, of which 29 failed to return.

50 Squadron

Urquhart was posted to 'A' Flight of Lancaster-equipped No.50 Squadron at Swinderby, Lincolnshire, on August 24, 1942, with Squadron Leader Moore as his pilot. Their first op together, just four days later, was an eight-hour round trip to Nuremberg in which most of the bombs fell short of the main target.

Multiple operations followed, including the raid on the Schneider factory at Le Creusot on October 17, 1942. This famous attack was carried out in daylight at low level, against a factory believed to be producing tanks, armoured cars and heavy guns. Some 94 Lancasters set out at midday, led by 49 Sqn's Wing Commander Slee. Without fighter escort, the force crossed the coast between La Rochelle and St Nazaire, going on to drop 140 tons of bombs from 2,500ft (762m). Unfortunately most of the bombs missed the target, although the only casualty was an aircraft from 61 Squadron. The raid involved a round trip of more than ten hours.

Pilot Officer Urquhart continued operations at a frantic pace and on December 17 flew a sortie to Soltau with a new crew. Their Lancaster was piloted by Sqn Ldr Birch, with Flying Officer Richard Trevor-Roper (Gibson's rear gunner on the dams raid) as one of the gunners. On their way home light flak batteries opened up on them, and they were attacked by a Junkers Ju 88 night fighter from below, causing extensive damage to the bomb bay and putting one of the engines out of action. Urquhart was injured, but continued to navigate with accuracy.

On landing they found out that the braking system was damaged, causing them to overshoot the runway. In his logbook, Urquhart noted: "The Lancaster had over 100 holes in the fuselage, some as big as 'Bofor' shells."

New Year, New Crew

In the New Year, Urquhart teamed up with another new crew, headed by pilot Flight Lieutenant Henry 'Hank' Maudslay, who was educated at Eton and a fine athlete; he had been awarded the DFC a year earlier while attached to 44 Squadron. Urquhart would stay with this crew until that fateful night of May 16/17, 1943, when they were shot down.

The crew opened their 1943 account with a raid on Essen on January 21. Sorties to Dusseldorf, Hamburg, Cologne, Turin, Wilhelmshaven, Lorient, Milan, Hamburg (again), Munich, Essen (again) and St Nazaire followed. The latter was F/O Urquhart's 28th op, for a total flying time of 497 hours, 182 of them on operations.

By this time, the crew had had also completed many night flying exercises, which included low flying. This vast operational experience obviously helped Flight Lieutenant Maudslay be selected by Wing Commander Guy Gibson for his secret new squadron at Scampton. When they heard the news, the whole crew volunteered to go with him, even though they were due a rest, having completed a 'tour'. Now officer commanding 50 Squadron, Wg Cdr Peter Birch endorsed Urquhart's logbook: "One of this squadron's most exceptional navigators, keen and efficient."

617 Squadron

Flight Lieutenant Maudslay and crew were posted to Scampton on March 25, 1943 to join the newly formed 617 Squadron. 'Hank' was immediately promoted to Squadron Leader and became 'B' Flight commander. Gibson had handpicked him for both his excellence as a pilot and his leadership skills, and he would play a prominent role in Operation Chastise aircrew training. Urquhart eventually became flight navigator for 'B' Flight, in training and on the raid.

Maudslay's crew took their first flight on March 31, in a Lancaster borrowed from IX(B) Squadron. It was a low-level cross-country exercise at 240mph (386km/h) for 3 hours, sometimes dropping down to 100ft (30m). None of the crews knew the purpose of this low flying, just that they had to perfect it.

On April 4, Maudslay and Urquhart flew Lancaster W4296/AJ-Z to Farnborough, where they stayed until the 9th while modifications were made, including fitting two Aldis lamps. On their return, Maudslay and Urquhart made two test runs across the aerodrome, »

▲ Guy Gibson wrote this letter to Robert Urquhart's mother, urging her not to give up hope for his survival as a prisoner of war. *via Simon Muggleton*

▲ Robert Urquhart's fellow Canadians on 617 Sqn were, back row, from left: Sgts S Oancia, FE Sutherland and HE O'Brien, Flt Sgts KW Brown, HA Weeks, JW Thrasher and GA Deering, Sgt WG Radcliffe, Flt Sgt DA Mclean, Flt Lt JC McCarthy (an American in RCAF service) and Flt Sgt GS McDonald. Sgt PE Pigeon, P/O HT Taerum, F/O DR Walker, Sgt CB Gowrie and F/O JA Rodger are in the front row. Fred Sutherland is one of the three veterans commemorating the 70th anniversary of the raid. RAF (AHB)/© UK MoD Crown Copyright 2023

using the new 'Spotlight Altimeter Calibrator'. That evening they repeated the tests at Skegness and over the Wash, showing that they could successfully keep to the required height.

Training continued in earnest and on April 24 they took Lancaster 'AJ-X' down to 60ft (18m) at 220mph (354km/h). The squadron medical officer, Flying Officer MW Arthurton, came along on the sortie, suffering the unpleasant side effect of continuous low flying – airsickness.

To the Dams

On May 11, Sqn Ldr Maudslay took off from Scampton in Lancaster 'AJ-X', complete with an inert Upkeep, which he dropped over the sea off Reculver, Kent, for the first time.

The next day, Maudslay and crew flew down to Reculver for a similar exercise. On this occasion, however, Maudslay flew below the required 60ft, dropping his Upkeep too low, which resulted in 'AJ-X's' tailplane being extensively damaged by spray. The aircraft could not be repaired, leaving only 19 aircraft available for the 21 crews trained up for Operation Chastise.

On May 13, all the 617 Sqn crews took part in a full dress rehearsal for the still-secret raid, on Uppingham Lake and Colchester reservoir. Maudslay and crew flew 'AJ-Z', again accompanied by the medical officer, this time with airsickness tablets! F/O Arthurton later recalled: "We took off at 21:50hrs and flew for four hours. I have not the foggiest notion where we were, nor exactly what we were doing, except we were flying low."

At 18:00 on May 15, Gibson briefed his two Flight Commanders, Young and Maudslay, along with Hopgood and Hay, revealing the purpose for the training. Over the next day, groundcrew prepared the 19 aircraft for that night's operation and at 18:00 the final aircrew briefing took place. Standing in front of a large map, Gibson announced: "Tonight you are going to attack the great dams in Germany." He then outlined the general plan of attack, with details of routes, call signs, codewords, weather conditions and ammunition loads.

By 21:00 all the crews were at their respective stations aboard the aircraft and at 21:28 the first Lancaster, 'AJ-E', took off. Sqn Ldr Maudslay took off at 21:59 in 'AJ-Z' (Zebra), in company with (B-Baker) and (N-Nuts), forming a V-formation in company with six other Lancasters, led by Gibson in 'AJ-G', as the first wave.

Against the Eder

Maudslay made the third attempt on the Eder dam at 01:45 on May 17. As he ran in, Gibson noticed something hanging down below Maudslay's Lancaster, then saw him level out, flying very fast, with his spotlights flickering on the water. Unfortunately, the bomb aimer, P/O Mike Fuller, released the Upkeep too late. Gibson later recalled: "It bounced and hit the parapet of the dam and exploded with a slow yellow, vivid flame, which lit up the whole valley like daylight for just a few seconds."

A red Very light went up at the same time, indicating that the aircraft had cleared the dam, but the blast almost certainly damaged 'AJ-Z'. Gibson called Maudslay over the radio: "Hello Z-Zebra are you all right?"

There was no answer. He called again, and an incredibly faint reply was heard from Maudslay: "I think so, stand by."

Meanwhile, Warrant Officer Cottam, 'AJ-Z's' wireless operator, sent a message at 01:57: "Gonner 28 B." (The code for mine released, overshot dam, no apparent breach.) It was the last message from Z-Zebra.

Sometime around 02:30, the crippled 'AJ-Z' was nearing Emmerich (an oil refining centre), when it was spotted by a light anti-aircraft post. Although they had strict orders not to fire on passing aircraft (so as not to give away the town's location) the gunners could not resist opening up on a British bomber flying low and on fire. Luftwaffe records show that the aircraft was hit at 02:36 and crashed southeast of Emmerich at Netterden, just 1.2 miles (2km) inside the German border. There were no survivors. It had taken Maudslay 50 minutes to fly the 140 miles (225km) from the Eder dam, probably because of the heavy damage sustained over the target.

The German authorities buried the crew in Dusseldorf, but on September 2, 1948, the Commonwealth War Graves Commission reinterred their remains in the Reichswald Forest War Cemetery. Robert Urquhart is buried in a joint grave (5B 16-18) with P/O Fuller and F/O Tytherleigh, the mid-upper gunner. The graves of Sqn Ldr Maudslay, W/O Cottam, Sgt Marriott, the flight engineer, and Sgt Burrows, rear gunner, are located behind them, in Graves 5C 1-4.

Urquhart's Observer flying logbook entries for May were endorsed by Flt Lt 'Micky' Martin, OC 'B' Flight, the final entry reading: "Ops-Eder Dam-Missing."

DAMBUSTERS 617 SQUADRON | 67

False Hope

Wing Commander Gibson wrote to Urquhart's mother on May 20, 1943 (as he did to all relatives of missing crew) giving her hope that Robert may have baled out and was perhaps a prisoner of war. By August 3, however, the RCAF had officially recognised that 'AJ-Z's' crew had been killed in action, and Urquhart's death was registered by the authorities in British Columbia on October 30, 1943.

On July 20, 1945, the *London Gazette* announced that Flying Officer Robert Alexander Urquhart had been awarded the Distinguished Flying Cross. In fact, the recommendation had originally been made by OC 50 Squadron on March 20, 1943, and endorsed by AVM Cochrane on May 4. Unfortunately, due to the exigencies of war, the paperwork was 'lost' until the closing stages of the war.

▲ Flying Officer Robert Urquhart's logbook entries for May 1943 were completed and endorsed by Flt Lt Harold 'Micky' Martin.
▼ Urquhart's logbook entries for April record 617 Sqn's work up for its first raid. The pages are endorsed by Guy Gibson and 'Hank' Maudslay. **both via Simon Muggleton**

AFTER THE DAMS
Lancaster to Tornado

With just one raid, No.617 Squadron had moved the nation, boosted morale throughout the Royal Air Force and delivered a blow of devastating immediacy and long-term inconvenience to Nazi Germany. It would henceforth be known as the 'Dambusters' and the decision was made to retain it as a 'special' unit for attacks falling outside the regular Main Force target set.

King George VI, accompanied by the Queen, visited RAF Scampton on May 27, 1943 and, with Wing Commander Gibson and the station commander, Group Captain John Whitworth, as escorts, talked with 617 Sqn's crews. The King examined aerial reconnaissance photographs of the breached dams and Gibson asked that he approve the squadron's motto and choose a badge from a selection of designs prepared by squadron members.

Gibson's Victoria Cross was one of 33 decorations awarded to aircrew for the dams raid, but a period of relative inactivity followed while the squadron regrouped

The Dambusters followed their opening action with an outstanding series of wartime precision strikes using revolutionary tactics and new weapons. Post-war the squadron served on the front line through the V-Bomber era, before re-equipping with the Tornado for an important role in the 1991 Gulf War

and re-equipped, morale declining as the commanding officer himself sank into depression. Meanwhile, standard Lancaster BI and BIII bombers began arriving, while some of the Type 464 (Provisioning) aircraft were de-modified.

On the night of July 15/16, 1943, the unit returned to combat, striking at railway electrical transformer units at San Polo d'Enza as part of an ongoing campaign against the Italian transport system. After attacking the target in northern Italy with 8,000lb (3,629kg) High Capacity (HC) bombs, the Lancasters recovered into Blida, North Africa, returning to Scampton on July 24/25, via a strike on the docks at Leghorn. By now Gibson had been posted away and Squadron Leader George Holden was in command when the squadron moved to RAF Coningsby in August.

RAF Coningsby
The first of 617 Sqn's notable raids from Coningsby was mounted against the Dortmund-Ems Canal on September 15/16, 1943. The new 12,000lb (5,440kg) HC bomb was chosen to arm the eight aircraft involved in the attack.

It comprised three Cookies linked together to produce a weapon largely unsuitable for such a target. Five aircraft were lost and with them the CO was killed,

◀ Groundcrew work with a Grand Slam.
617 Sqn Archive/© UK MoD Crown Copyright 2023

▼ A toned-down anti-flash white 617 Sqn Vulcan B2A carries a Blue Steel training round.
© UK MoD Crown Copyright 2023

▲ The modifications necessary to accommodate Grand Slam resulted in the Lancaster BI (Special). **Pete West**

▲ The Petwood Hotel at Woodhall Spa was adopted as the 617 Sqn officers' mess. Today it holds an impressive array of Dambusters memorabilia. **Petwood Hotel**

▶ The twin railway viaducts at Bielefeld were attacked with a Grand Slam on March 14, 1945. **617 Sqn Archive/© UK MoD Crown Copyright 2023**

along with four members of Gibson's original dams raid crew.

Nevertheless, the squadron was able to put up a force against the Antheor viaduct, another transport target, this time on the Franco-Italian border, the following night, but again with little success. The squadron's replacement CO was Wing Commander Leonard Cheshire and soon he was leading a series of precision attacks, many of them against the V1 flying bomb launch sites that began appearing all over the Pas de Calais.

Small and well concealed targets, the V1 installations led Cheshire to develop his own techniques for low-level target marking, at first using a standard Lancaster. He would fly in ahead of the squadron, identifying and marking the target, often in the face of extreme opposition, before climbing to circle and act as master bomber once the attack was underway.

Later he realised that a smaller, nimble aircraft would be more suitable as a low-level target marker and the squadron employed Mosquitos, Lockheed P-38 Lightnings and North American Mustangs in the role. Number 617 Sqn's reputation for navigation and bombing accuracy continued to grow and after a raid conducted in his familiar fashion against heavy defences at Munich in summer 1944, Cheshire was awarded the Victoria Cross for his continued bravery in action.

RAF Woodhall Spa

In January 1944, Number 617 Sqn made the very short hop from RAF Coningsby to nearby Woodhall Spa. There it remained until June 1945, Cheshire commanding until July 1944, when Wing Commander JB 'Willie' Tait took over as boss.

Several precision bombing sorties were flown from Woodhall Spa, but one operation stands out for its brilliance, although not a single bomb was dropped. Over the »

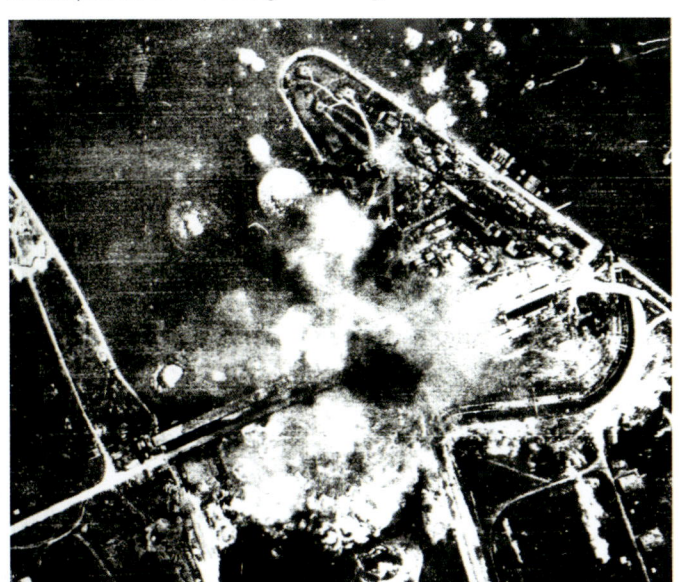

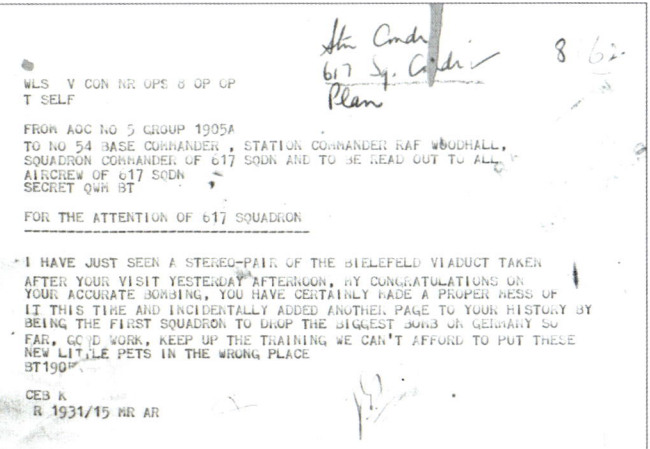

▲ AOC 5 Gp sent his appreciation of the Bielefeld attack via telegram on March 15, 1945.
◀ Tallboys destroyed the gates of the Kembs barrage in October 1944. **both 617 Sqn Archive/© UK MoD Crown Copyright 2023**

night of June 5/6, 1944, a group of 18 small vessels moved towards the French coast at 7kt (13km/h) as part of Operation Taxable. Overhead, 617 Sqn's Lancasters flew precise tracks, dropping bundles of 'window' (chaff) at timed intervals to give the surface craft the radar signature of a much larger invasion fleet. Over 3.5 hours, the aircrafts' oval flight paths moved imperceptibly towards France, matching the 7kt advance of the vessels below and successfully spoofing the German defences while the actual invasion force landed 100 miles (160km) away.

▲ This Lancaster BVII formation was over Benares, India, in 1946. The squadron abandoned its original 'AJ' codes during World War II, replacing them with 'KC', although the Tallboy and Grand Slam aircraft wore 'YZ'. The 'AJ' codes later returned on the Tornado. **Andrew Thomas**

▲ *Tirpitz* capsized in Alten fjord. **617 Sqn Archive/© UK MoD Crown Copyright 2013**

Tirpitz
Germany's 45,000-ton battleship *Tirpitz* had remained a threat in the North Atlantic, evading all attempts at its destruction. Numbers IX(B) and 617 Sqns had worked together on precision strikes through the summer of 1944 and in September they were ordered against the battleship.

Moored in Norway's Kaa fjord, the ship was beyond the Lancasters' reach and 38 aircraft modified with long-range tanks and carrying the ordnance needed for the attack, departed for Yagavik, USSR. From there the target was more easily in range and on September 15 the combined force dropped Tallboys and 'Johnny Walker' anti-shipping mines against the vessel.

A single Tallboy hit was scored, causing the Germans to move *Tirpitz* to Tromsø for repair, although the RAF crews were unaware of this as they returned to their temporary Soviet base. Now moored in Alten fjord, off Tromsø island, *Tirpitz* was within range of a strike from Lossiemouth, and IX(B) and 617 Sqns despatched Lancasters to the Moray station for another attack on October 29. This time they scored no hits as cloud cover obscured the target.

A third mission was flown on November 12, again from Lossiemouth. This time visibility was excellent and although fighters were scrambled to intercept, they were directed to Kaa fjord in error. The ship was hit by a number of Tallboys, before being rocked by a huge explosion and capsizing, with the loss of around 1,000 souls.

▶▼ Telegrams from Barnes Wallis and Lord Trenchard, 'father of the RAF'. both 617 Sqn Archive/© UK MoD Crown Copyright 2023

Operations in support of D-Day and the Allied advance into Europe continued with an attack against the Saumur railway tunnel in northern France, on June 8/9, 1944. The successful operation used another of Barnes Wallis's special weapons for the first time, the 12,000lb Tallboy.

Tallboys and Grand Slam
Tait was in command when 617 Sqn joined forces with IX(B) Sqn, for an attack on the battleship *Tirpitz* in September 1944. The squadrons had to return to the ship twice more, but in the meantime the Dambusters went dam busting again.

The Kembs dam in southern Germany was a barrage-type dam, consisting of lock gates and interconnecting piers to control the water. It was successfully struck with Tallboys on October 7/8, 1944, for the loss of two Lancasters.

On March 14, 1945, Wallis's 10-ton bomb finally became an operational reality, when 617 Sqn dropped one of his 22,000lb (9,979kg) Grand Slam weapons against the Bielefeld railway viaduct in Germany, taking it out of commission for the rest of the war. More Grand Slams and Tallboys were expended against targets requiring the particular accuracy of 617 Sqn and the destructive power of these monster weapons.

The unit's final target of the war was Hitler's Berchtesgaden retreat in the Bavarian Alps, which was attacked using Tallboys.

Tiger Force
With the end of the war in Europe, 617 Sqn moved to RAF Waddington in June, preparing itself for Lancaster operations as part of the RAF's Tiger Force. Assembled for action against Japanese forces in the Pacific, Tiger Force was to operate Lancasters as an interim measure, while the longer-ranged Lincoln was brought into service.

The Pacific war ended in August 1945, but 617 Sqn continued with a deployment to Salbani, India, in January 1946. It returned its

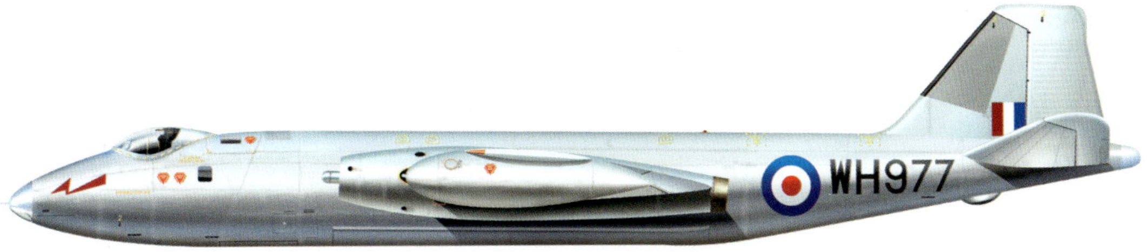

▲ English Electric Canberra B6 WH977 served 617 Sqn as part of the Binbrook Wing. All of the Wing's Canberras wore lightning bolts, those of the Dambusters being in red. **Pete West**

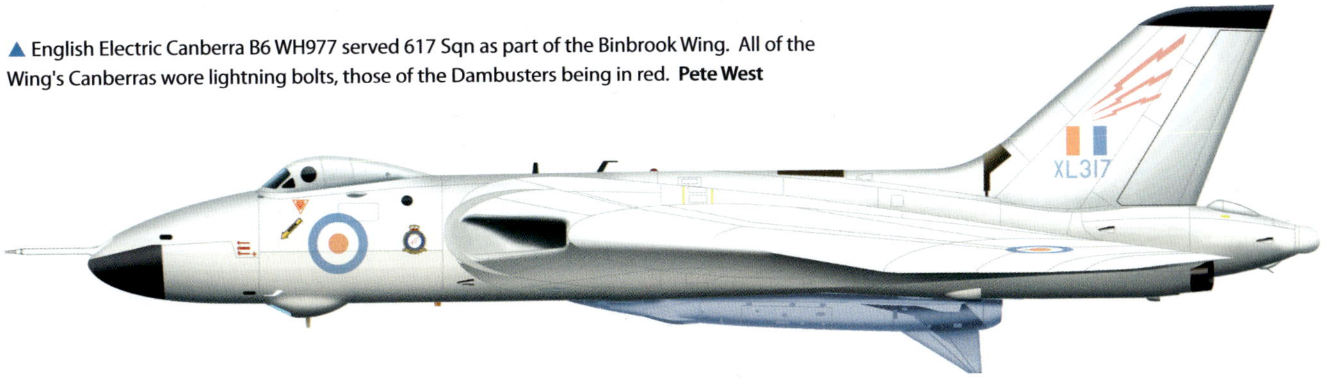

▲ Avro Vulcan B2A XL317, wears the anti-flash white/toned-down markings scheme. Blue Steel-compatible Vulcans were formally designated B2A. Blue Steel itself had a range of around 115 miles (185km) when launched from altitude, reaching a maximum speed of Mach 2.3 and delivering its nuclear warhead in a Mach 1.5+ dive. **Pete West**

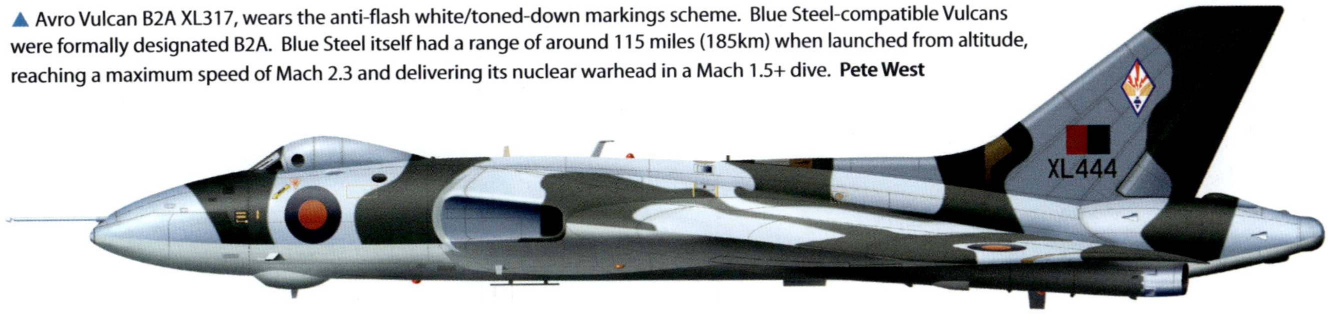

▲ Avro Vulcan B2 XL444, wears the green/grey camouflage over light grey that was among the schemes adopted for low-level work. The antenna below the engine nacelle is part of the ECM equipment fitted to provide a degree of self protection. **Pete West**

▲ Low-level over the desert in training for Desert Storm. Crews from 617 Sqn were among those who made daring low-level attacks on Iraqi airfields. **617 Sqn Archive/© UK MoD Crown Copyright 2023**

new Lancaster BVII bombers to the UK in May, this time taking up station at RAF Binbrook to re-equip with Lincolns.

A goodwill tour of the US and Canada followed in 1947, the squadron making the RAF's first direct transatlantic crossing in the process. In 1950 the Dambusters used their Lincolns to win the annual Bomber Command bombing competition and the Laurence Minot Trophy.

Canberras and V-Force

Number 617 Squadron became the RAF's second jet bomber squadron in 1952, when it traded its Lincolns for English Electric Canberras. It deployed to Butterworth, Malaysia in 1955, attacking Communist guerrillas during the Malayan Emergency. After four months of operations it returned to Binbrook and disbanded on December 15.

When RAF Scampton reopened in 1958, after redevelopment as a V-Bomber base, 617 Sqn was the first unit to take up residence, reforming on the Avro Vulcan at its original home, on May 1. Trophies and recognition from bombing competitions soon followed and as well as maintaining nuclear alert with its Blue Danube-armed »

Vulcans, the squadron managed a record-breaking flight to Australia in June 1961.

Squadron Leader Beavis flew a Vulcan B1A direct from Scampton to Sydney, covering the 11,500 miles (18,500km) in 20 hours 3 minutes, including three aerial refuellings.

The Vulcan had been designed to penetrate enemy airspace at speeds and altitudes beyond those of contemporary fighters, but this tactic became irrelevant on May 1, 1960, when a Soviet surface-to-air missile (SAM) downed a CIA Lockheed U-2 over the USSR. Avro's Blue Steel stand-off missile was already in development, however, becoming operational on 617 Sqn's new Vulcan B2 bombers in February 1963.

Blue Steel provided a degree of protection, but striking targets deeper in the USSR would still bring the Vulcans within SAM range. Blue Steel was modified for low-level delivery, but this compromised its range and in 1968 the weapon was withdrawn.

Along with the remaining Vulcan units, 617 Sqn continued in a low-level bombing role, using conventional weapons as well as the WE.177 nuclear store. With the drawdown of the Vulcan force, the Dambusters disbanded again on December 31, 1981.

Tornado

For the first time in its history, No.617 Sqn moved out of Lincolnshire, when it began receiving the Tornado GR1 at RAF Marham, Norfolk, in April 1982. Declared operational again on May 16, 1983, exactly 40 years since Operation Chastise, the squadron was soon winning more trophies, this time in the US, much to the chagrin of Strategic Air Command's Boeing B-52 Stratofortress squadrons.

Number 617 Squadron was the RAF's second operational Tornado unit and its crews were in the vanguard of the Tornado personnel despatched to the Persian Gulf in response to Iraq's 1990 invasion of Kuwait. In particular, OC 617 Sqn, Wing Commander Bob Iveson, led the initial deployment, known as No.617 Squadron (Composite), although it later became the Tornado Detachment under OC 16 Sqn. Iveson then took command of a small flight comprising 13 and 617 Sqn crews and dedicated to using the new Thermal Imaging Airborne Laser Designator (TIALD) targeting pod.

▶ Sea Eagle was a large weapon, most likely to have been employed in combat as a pair per aircraft. Complex tactics were developed for its use, and the weapon had a range in excess of 57 miles (92km). **Key Collection**

In the years that followed the 1991 Gulf War, 617 Sqn took its turn policing the northern and southern no-fly zones over Iraq, Operations Warden and Jural, respectively. Its primary mission, however, became maritime attack, using the Sea Eagle missile.

On April 27, 1994, the squadron returned to Lossiemouth – 'Lossie'. After more than a decade at RAF Marham, the Dambusters had received the first of their dedicated Tornado GR1B aircraft on April 14. The Scottish station, sitting prominently on the Moray coast, north of Elgin, was far better positioned than Marham for the Tornados to counter the perceived maritime threat, but in the event the anti-ship role was relatively short lived.

While the Sea Eagle was briefly 617's primary weapon and its delivery against shipping targets its lead role, it also maintained an overland capability. This allowed it to take its turn on Operation Warden during 1995, operating over northern Iraq out of Incirlik, Turkey, and relieving a Harrier detachment.

The first of the Dambuster's Tornado GR4 jets arrived at Lossiemouth in 2000 and with the maritime role in abeyance, the squadron began working up on its new equipment..

▲ It was very much in keeping with its reputation for innovation that 617 Sqn should be home to the RAF's first female combat pilot. Flt Lt Jo Salter was photographed flying this GR1B in February 1995, during the era in which 617 Sqn's jets adopted the 'AJ' codes of Word War II. **Key Collection**

▲ Two 617 Squadron Tornado GR4s received 70th anniversary schemes in 2013. **Jamie Hunter/Aviacom**

▲▶ The modern 617 Sqn badge includes the Queen's crown. © UK MoD Crown Copyright 2023

▼ Fading light adds to the drama of a 617 Sqn GR4 launch from Kandahar in June 2011. Equipped with Paveway IV, a Litening III pod and its internal cannon, this aircraft represented a versatile attack and reconnaissance capability in the armed overwatch role. Sgt Ross Tilly/© UK MoD Crown Copyright 2023

Operation Telic

Early in 2003, a Coalition of forces began assembling for an invasion of Iraq. Under the US codename Operation Iraqi Freedom, the UK's Operation Telic was a vital component in the response to the Iraqi leadership's flouting of UN resolutions. RAF Tornados deployed to Ali Al Salem, Kuwait and Al Udeid, Qatar, 617 Sqn jets and crews joining those from II(AC), IX(B), 13 and 31 Sqns in Kuwait.

A handful of Urgent Operational Requirements resulted in a series of modifications to the deployed jets, among them an interim Storm Shadow capability. Number 617 Squadron was tasked with rapidly clearing the weapon for operational use and on March 3, 2003, in the month of its 60th anniversary, the squadron debuted the cruise missile in combat.

Wing Commander Dave Robertson, Officer Commanding 617 Sqn at the time, led the first Storm Shadow mission and although it met with considerable success, he reported that the aircraft had encountered heavy AAA (anti-aircraft artillery) and that one of his pilots had been forced to jettison drop tanks as he scrambled for more manoeuvrability to defeat a surface-to-air missile threat.

With the early combat phase of Telic over, Tornado deployments to the region continued in support of Coalition ground forces. The Dambusters took their turn manning these detachments at Al Udeid with the other front-line squadrons, in a rotating task that lasted until 2009.

Operation Herrick

Although 617 Sqn was not the first to deploy its Tornados to Kandahar under Operation Herrick, it took its turn in the regular movement of aircraft and personnel into Afghanistan. When the Tornado Force engaged in Operation Ellamy over Libya in 2011, 617 Sqn was fulfilling the commitment to Herrick, leaving it little opportunity to contribute to the new operation.

Lossie then provided an extra rotation through Kandahar, since the Marham squadrons were involved in and recovering from Libya operations, so that 617 Sqn returned to Afghanistan just five and a half months after coming home. In effect, aircrew returned, recovered, then dived straight back into work-up to redeploy. Nevertheless, the Dambusters still managed to supply crews for Ellamy Storm Shadow attacks.

In its 70th anniversary year the squadron prepared for and deployed on its final Herrick tour, working up and refining the skillsets needed for the close air support and reconnaissance missions before delivering them on behalf of Coalition commanders.

Then Officer Commanding 617 Sqn, Wing Commander David Arthurton explained how the unit planned its training regime within the cycle of Afghanistan deployments. "After returning from Afghanistan, the squadron flies a reset package to get the aircrews and engineers back into UK methods of working. On operations, tasks tend to be fairly similar day in and day out, but at home there's a much broader spectrum of activity, including Storm Shadow, which is a niche Tornado GR4 role, but represents some of our high-end capability.

"Then there's night-vision goggle flying and getting crews qualified at low level on those. The training is rigorous and currency flying is required to ensure that crews remain proficient."

1943 vs 2013

In 1943, 617 Sqn launched a modest force of Lancasters against what would today be described as 'hard' targets – dams with reinforced structures. Again in modern terms, the aircraft ingressed to the target area at low level in the hope of avoiding enemy defences, the survivors egressing as best they could to get home safely. They planned their routes, bomb runs and tactics using pre-war documentation and intelligence collected by unarmed Spitfire photo-reconnaissance aircraft.

Asked how 617 might attack a hard target at a similar range with the Tornado, Wg Cdr Arthurton's plan revealed similarities with 1943, but also illustrated the step change in capabilities through 70 years of tactical and technological development.

"We'd look at the task first. What effect do we want to achieve on the target? Are we trying to destroy it? Do we want to hamper its use and cause disruption in the target area, or do we simply want to send a message to say, 'We can destroy this if we want to'?"

▲ The 65th anniversary of the dams raid was marked in 2008 by a pair of 617 Sqn Tornados flying over the Derwent dam. The Royal Air Force Battle of Britain Memorial Flight's Lancaster also overflew the dam and reservoir. Sgt Graham Spark/© UK MoD Crown Copyright 2023

Told that the intention is to drop a span of an imaginary bridge, he continued: "We'd look at the target, paying attention to its physical construction and use operational analysis to help determine how to attack it. The analysis would try to identify a weak link in the structure, or some vulnerable point that would create the desired effect, but not too much. We've found increasingly that it's very easy to take bridges down, but when you're trying to stabilise a population and move supplies into a region, you've scored an own goal if you've removed the infrastructure that's going to enable that next part of the operation.

"We'd also examine the defences around the target to see whether we can attack it on our own or whether we need to be part of a package. Based on threat, target construction and the effect we want to achieve, we'd come up with the best course of action. The package supporting us would also have an influence. For example, do we have an air-refuelling capability? If it's limited, then Storm Shadow is a useful weapon, for example. Is the target defended by fighters? Do we have assets that can provide sweep and escort to allow us to ingress and keep all our weapons on the aircraft until we're ready to drop them?

"All this analysis would drive the tactics employed. One of our qualified weapons instructors – the squadron's tactical experts – would work on the tactics with the aircrew. In training we'd then try the mission and use feedback from the debrief to tweak the tactics, although in a war there may not be the opportunity to re-attack." The result of such training was a 'catalogue' of tactics and experience to be dipped into, adopted and adapted as required for combat operations or peacetime exercises.

Intelligence for the theoretical bridge drop would have come to the squadron as a 'targeting pack' from the Targeting Cell in the Air Operations Centre. Containing data from a number of sources, including the RAF's own constellation of ISTAR assets, it may also have included information from coalition partners. Clearly vital before an attack, target intelligence is also crucial after a strike, in the final assessment of whether the raid was effective.

If an attacking aircraft was equipped with a Litening III pod, then instantaneous battle damage assessment was possible, but it deprived the jet of a weapon and its utility had to be considered on a mission-by-mission basis. If bombs were being dropped through cloud, the pod was of little benefit anyway and bombing on GPS-quality coordinates would be preferred.

Of course, no bridges needed to be attacked during 617 Sqn's last operational deployment with the Tornado. It returned home from Afghanistan in February 2014 and disbanded on March 28, ready to reform on the F-35B, back at RAF Marham.

▲ Marked for 617 Sqn, the Royal Air Force Memorial Flight Lancaster flies with a squadron Tornado. The formation was not easy to fly, the Lancaster cruising not much faster than the speed at which the Tornado usually landed. **Richard Paver**

The fins of the 70th anniversary Tornados featured a representation of the squadron badge, in which the three lightning flashes represent the Möhne, Eder and Sorpe. Silhouettes of the Tornado and Type 464 (Provisioning) Lancaster adorned the rudder, while the forward fuselage bore standard squadron markings. **Jamie Hunter/Aviacom**

▲ At Lossie, reminders of 617 Sqn's illustrious past included this WE.177 bomb casing. **SAC Connor Payne/© UK MoD Crown Copyright 2023**

Key Books MAIL ORDER

METEOR — NEW

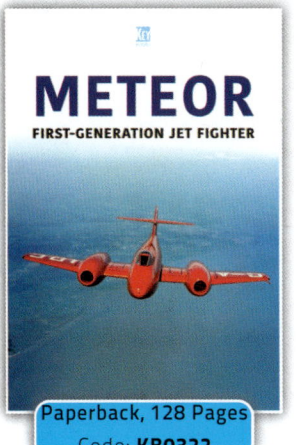

Paperback, 128 Pages
Code: KB0322

Historic Military Aircraft Series, Vol. 30

This new book edition of Aeroplane Icons: Meteor tracks the design and development, service and variants of Britain's first jet fighter.

ONLY £16.99

Subscribers call for your £2 discount

VICKERS VISCOUNT — NEW

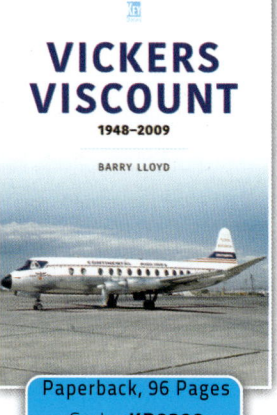

Paperback, 96 Pages
Code: KB0299

Historic Commercial Aircraft Series, Vol. 16

With more than 140 historic black and white and colour photographs, this volume offers a comprehensive guide to one of the most popular passenger aircraft.

ONLY £16.99

Subscribers call for your £2 discount

BLENHEIM — NEW

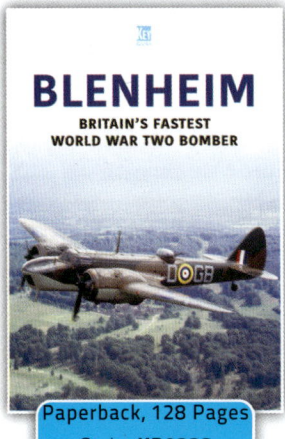

Paperback, 128 Pages
Code: KB0323

Historic Military Aircraft Series, Vol. 31

This new book edition of Aeroplane Icons: Blenheim showcases this incredible aircraft and celebrates its ground-breaking history.

ONLY £16.99

Subscribers call for your £2 discount

SOUTH AMERICAN PROPS — NEW

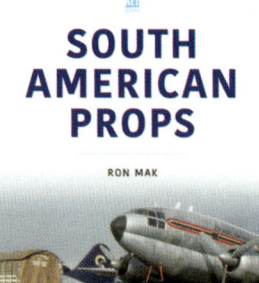

Paperback, 96 Pages
Code: KB0269

Historic Military Aircraft Series, Vol. 15

Highly illustrated with over 200 colour images, this book features photos from airports in Venezuela, Suriname, Brazil, Paraguay, Uruguay, Argentina, Chile, Bolivia, Peru, Ecuador and Colombia.

ONLY £16.99

Subscribers call for your £2 discount

CURTISS 1907 - 47

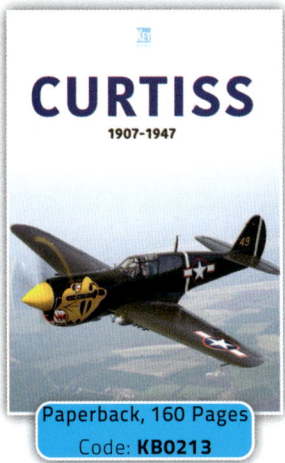

Paperback, 160 Pages
Code: KB0213

Aviation Industry Series, Vol. 6

This new book edition of Aeroplane's Curtiss Company Profile 1907 – 1947 showcases the aircraft of Curtiss and its contribution to history.

ONLY £17.99

Subscribers call for your £2 discount

LUFTWAFFE FIGHTERS OF WORLD WAR TWO

Paperback, 128 Pages
Code: KB0257

This book gives the reader, be they well-versed in Luftwaffe matters or just simply curious to know more, an insight into the main Luftwaffe fighters of World War Two.

ONLY £18.99

Subscribers call for your £2 discount

---

shop.keypublishing.com/books

Or call **UK: 01780 480404** - **Overseas: +44 1780 480404**

Monday to Friday 9am-5:30pm GMT. Free 2nd class P&P on all UK & BFPO orders. Overseas charges apply. All publication dates subject to change

TO VIEW OUR FULL RANGE OF BOOKS, VISIT OUR SHOP

THE TORNADO
Swing-Wing Backbone

The Tornado was the cornerstone of RAF offensive capabilities for almost four decades. Retired from service in March 2019, the upgraded GR4 was at the height of its considerable capability

On January 1, 1983, 617 Squadron 'The Dambusters' reformed as a Panavia Tornado GR1 unit, after 23 years on the Avro Vulcan. It was the second RAF squadron to re-equip on the type, taking on an aircraft that was based on what its multinational manufacturing organisation called the Tornado IDS (Interdictor Strike). The RAF-optimised Tornado GR1 was expected to take on the roles of interdiction – effectively the destruction of targets behind enemy lines, such as transport infrastructure, airfields, ammunition dumps and troop concentrations. It also took the strike role, which for the Cold War RAF was specifically a nuclear mission, using the WE.177 bomb.

Ambitious from the outset, the Tornado programme combined an advanced airframe with new, technologically superior engines and a comprehensive avionics fit, allowing high-speed, low-level penetration to heavily defended targets in all weathers and at night. Development work had begun in the mid-1960s, under a multi-national agreement that the UK joined after the BAC TSR.2 programme was cancelled in 1968.

Panavia Aircraft GmbH was created in March 1969, with the UK, West Germany and Italy as signatories. The new consortium had responsibility for managing the design and development of the Tornado weapon system, while production and the development of prototypes fell to BAC (British Aircraft Corporation), Italy's Aeritalia and West Germany' MBB (Messerschmitt-Bölkow-Blohm). The operational requirements of the signatory nations differed markedly at first, but resolution occurred in April 1970, resulting in the affirmation of a two-seat, variable-geometry aircraft with advanced capabilities in ground attack and interdiction.

World-Class Aircraft

From the outset, the Tornado was designed as a world-class combat aircraft. Its complex design was matched against a myriad of Cold War scenarios and threats. In essence, the Tornado has developed into a very capable attack aircraft capable of deep strike in all weathers, day and night. Of note, it was designed with computer systems that were upgradeable and as a result, operational flight programmes have marched in pace with technology and responded to changing »

◀ A large weapon, generally carried under the fuselage, Sea Eagle is carried alongside a pair of erstwhile Tornado F3 drop tanks on this 617 Sqn GR1B.
© UK MoD Crown Copyright 2023

▲ Wearing grey and green wraparound camouflage, this Tornado GR1 carries the markings of No.31 Squadron 'Goldstars'. It stood down in 2019. **Key Collection**

▼ This impressive line of Tornado GR1, IDS and F3 jets begins furthest away from the camera with GR1s from No.27 Sqn and No.45 Sqn/Tornado Weapons Conversion Unit, then a 17 Sqn GR1 sits between two German machines, followed by an Italian IDS, then GR1s from II(AC) Sqn and an unknown unit, although the aircraft's fin bears an unlikely F3 Operational Evaluation Unit marking. The last aircraft in the line are an Italian IDS and F3s from 11 Sqn, 229 OCU/65 Sqn and 29 Sqn. **Key Collection**

capability requirements. Today the Tornado GR4 still represents world-class combat capability, a remarkable achievement considering that the first flight of prototype P01 took place in August 1974 and that British Aerospace (BAe) rolled out the first production aircraft in June 1979.

Initial market analysis for the programme perceived a requirement for more than 1,000 aircraft, but initial orders ultimately amounted to 220 Tornado GR1s for the RAF, plus 324 Tornado IDS for the Luftwaffe and Marineflieger, and 100 for the Aeronautica Militare. To these numbers were later added the 165 Tornado ADV (Air Defence Variant (later F2 and F3)) aircraft for the RAF, and the aircraft of the only Tornado 'export' customer, Saudi Arabia. The Saudis eventually bought 96 IDS Tornados and 24 ADVs.

Tornado Enters Service

The first Tornado GR1 made its maiden flight in July 1979 and the final aircraft was delivered in March 1993. In total, 229 Tornado GR1 aircraft were delivered to the RAF and assigned to units based in the UK and West Germany. Aircrews were initially trained at the Tri-National Tornado Training Establishment at RAF Cottesmore, before completing weapons training at RAF Honington on the Tornado Weapons Conversion Unit.

Three operational squadrons were formed at RAF Honington and RAF Marham in 1982-83. With the role of developing the best operational tactics, the RAF established the Tornado Operational Evaluation Unit (TOEU), which became the Strike Attack Operational Evaluation Unit in 1983 and remains operational as 41(R) Sqn. Key work for the TOEU was the development of best procedures for target acquisition and attack with nuclear weapons.

As the cornerstone of RAF Germany (RAFG), the GR1 equipped seven squadrons based at RAF Brüggen and RAF Laarbruch, all assigned to the ground attack and reconnaissance roles; moreover, all of the

▼ Number 41(R) Sqn formed out of the Fast Jet Weapons Operational Evaluation Unit in 2004 and for a while flew the Harrier (lead), Tornado F3 (to port) and Tornado GR4. **SAC Graham Taylor/© UK MoD Crown Copyright 2023**

▲ British Aerospace rolled out the first production Tornado GR1 from its Warton facility on June 5, 1979. **British Aerospace/Key Collection**

squadrons were proficient in the nuclear role and trained to conduct strikes using WE.177 – squadrons held continuous quick reaction alert and provided a significant contribution to the UK Government's nuclear deterrence capability. The Tornado replaced the SEPECAT Jaguar and Blackburn Buccaneer in West Germany, considerably upgrading RAFG's striking power.

Needing a replacement for its maritime attack Buccaneer fleet, the RAF developed the Tornado GR1B, with weapons interfaces for as many as four Sea Eagle anti-shipping missiles; these aircraft were externally identical to a standard GR1 with the only modifications involving mission avionics and weapon mounts.

The modifications required to optimise the GR1 as a tactical reconnaissance platform were rather more radical, however, and the RAF developed the GR1A as a result. Fourteen GR1As, including the prototype, were produced by conversion from GR1 standard and 16 were built as such. The brown-coloured 'windows' in its forward fuselage sides easily identified the GR1A; these served a side-looking infrared sensor, while a fairing below the fuselage housed a panoramic infrared linescan. The model's attack and navigation systems remained largely unaltered, and it remained capable of routine attack missions.

The Tornado continued to provide a significant role in UK deterrence throughout the 1980s and 1990s until the introduction of the submarine-launched Trident missile and the subsequent end of the Cold War. WE.177 was retired in 1998 and RAF Germany's squadrons were progressively withdrawn through the 1990s, some disbanding and others finding new homes in the UK.

Mid-Life Update
The Tornado's combat debut came in 1991 with Operation Granby, the UK's contribution to the US-led Operation Desert Storm. A large Coalition had assembled to eject Iraqi forces from Kuwait after their August 2, 1990 invasion of the country. The RAF committed Tornado GR1, GR1A and F3 aircraft to the campaign and its GR1 attack aircraft were in action from the opening phase of combat on January 17, 1991.

The results were outstanding, but the experience also pointed to deficiencies in capability, especially when compared to the latest US warplanes and with regard to the RAF's changing requirements. It had procured Tornado as a low-level penetrator armed primarily with conventional and nuclear free-fall bombs, and while this capability remained relevant, the future of ground attack would require precision delivery of guided weapons.

Upgrades to the GR1 navigation and weapons systems lay at the core of the RAF's mid-life update (MLU) for the type. A laser-ranger and marked target seeker (LRMTS) had always been standard GR1 »

▼ Numbers 31, 17 and IX(B) Squadrons, represented here from front to back, formed the Brüggen Wing. No.31 Sqn was the last RAF squadron in Germany, transferring to RAF Marham in 2001. No.17 Sqn is now the F-35B OEU, while IX(B) operates the Typhoon at Lossiemouth. **© UK MoD Crown Copyright 2023**

'kit', but during Operation Granby, crews from 13 and 617 Squadrons had introduced the Thermal Imaging Airborne Laser Designator (TIALD) into service. With this new system the Tornado could designate targets for its own laser-guided bombs (LGBs) and the MLU brought full integration of TIALD and laid the foundations for future capability growth. The result was Tornado GR4, a far more capable aircraft that also boasted a forward-looking infrared (FLIR) and night-vision goggle (NVG) compatible cockpit.

Since the first GR4 was delivered back to the RAF in 1997, the aircraft's capabilities have been greatly expanded. The Litening III (LIII) targeting pod now delivers performance way beyond that possible with TIALD and in conjunction with the Paveway IV (with laser and GPS guidance) and Brimstone (in millimetre-wave (MMW) guided 'legacy' form, or as the Dual Mode Seeker (DMS) MMW and laser-guided version) precision-guided munitions (PGMs), provides unmatched capability. Storm Shadow, a turbojet-powered cruise missile is also a standard GR4 weapon, delivering precise, hard-hitting firepower from considerable ranges.

Interestingly, while the GR1A Tornados were upgraded to GR4A standard, the reconnaissance fit has been removed in favour of the considerably more capable Reconnaissance Pod Airborne for Tornado (RAPTOR). Another world-class sensor, RAPTOR allows real-time data linking with the ground, as well as conferring sub-strategic reconnaissance capability onto the essentially tactical Tornado airframe.

GR1 at War

For Operation Granby, practically all of RAF Germany's Tornado units were mobilised, with the first aircraft arriving in the Gulf in August 1990. Three squadrons were soon combat ready in Bahrain and another three, based in Saudi Arabia, were ready for war by the end of September.

Initial missions across a broad target set were carried out mainly by night and at low level. This tactic, however, soon proved to be excessively dangerous and 'carpet' AAA (anti-aircraft artillery) and SAMs (surface-to-air missiles) resulted in the loss of four aircraft. As a result, Allied Command decided to conduct attack missions from medium and high altitudes.

The 1991 Gulf War also saw the first use of the Air-Launched Anti-Radiation Missile (ALARM), despite the fact that the weapon had not been officially released for operational service. This was also the case with the TIALD designation pod, which cut its teeth as a capability during the conflict. Tornado GR1s conducted more that 1,500 operational sorties during Desert Storm, employing almost 100 JP233 runway denial weapons, and dropping 4,200 free-fall weapons and almost 1,000 LGBs. »

▼▶ With a RAPTOR pod under its fuselage, the Tornado GR4 was a world-class tactical reconnaissance platform. The system proved its immense utility over Afghanistan and was much envied among the Coalition partners over Libya in 2011. all © UK MoD Crown Copyright 2023

▼ Nose art quickly spread across the deployed Tornado fleet during Operation Granby. Some of the Muharraq-based aircraft were apparently assigned to 'Snoopy Airways', among them ZD790/D 'Debbie'. Others were ZA471/E 'Emma', ZA491/N 'Nikki', and ZD892/H 'Helen'. © UK MoD Crown Copyright 2023

The Names Behind Panavia – Tornado to Typhoon
Tornado production spanned a period of considerable consolidation within Europe's aviation industry and Panavia's constituent companies changed quite dramatically. The original UK partner was BAC, formed in 1960 to produce the TSR.2, by merging Bristol, English Electric and Vickers. Hunting was subsequently added to the group. Tornado first flew with BAC involvement, but British Aerospace rolled out the first production aircraft, having been produced through the merger of Hawker Siddeley and BAC in 1977. BAE Systems was formed out of BAe and Marconi in 1999 and continues to support RAF and Saudi Tornado operations, as well as being the UK's Eurofighter partner.

Fiat Aviazione and IRI-Finmeccanica formed Aeritalia in November 1969, absorbing the Aerfer and Salmoiraghi concerns in the process. In 1990 Aeritalia and Selenia merged to form Alenia Aeronautica, one of the Eurofighter partners. In 2012 the company was renamed Alenia Aermacchi.

Messerschmitt-Bölkow-Blohm resulted from a 1969 merger between Messerschmitt-Bölkow (itself a merger between the post-war Bölkow company and the famous Messerschmitt) and Hamburger Flugzeugbau (which built the wartime Blohm und Voss series of seaplanes). In 1989 Deutsche Aerospace (DASA) was formed to oversee the aerospace activities of the Daimler-Benz group, soon adding control of MBB to its portfolio. Later reorganised as DaimlerChrysler, in 2000 DASA combined with the French Aerospatiale-Matra and Spanish CASA organisations to form the European Aeronautic Defence And Space Company (EADS), effectively taking on both the Spanish and German responsibilities for the Eurofighter programme.

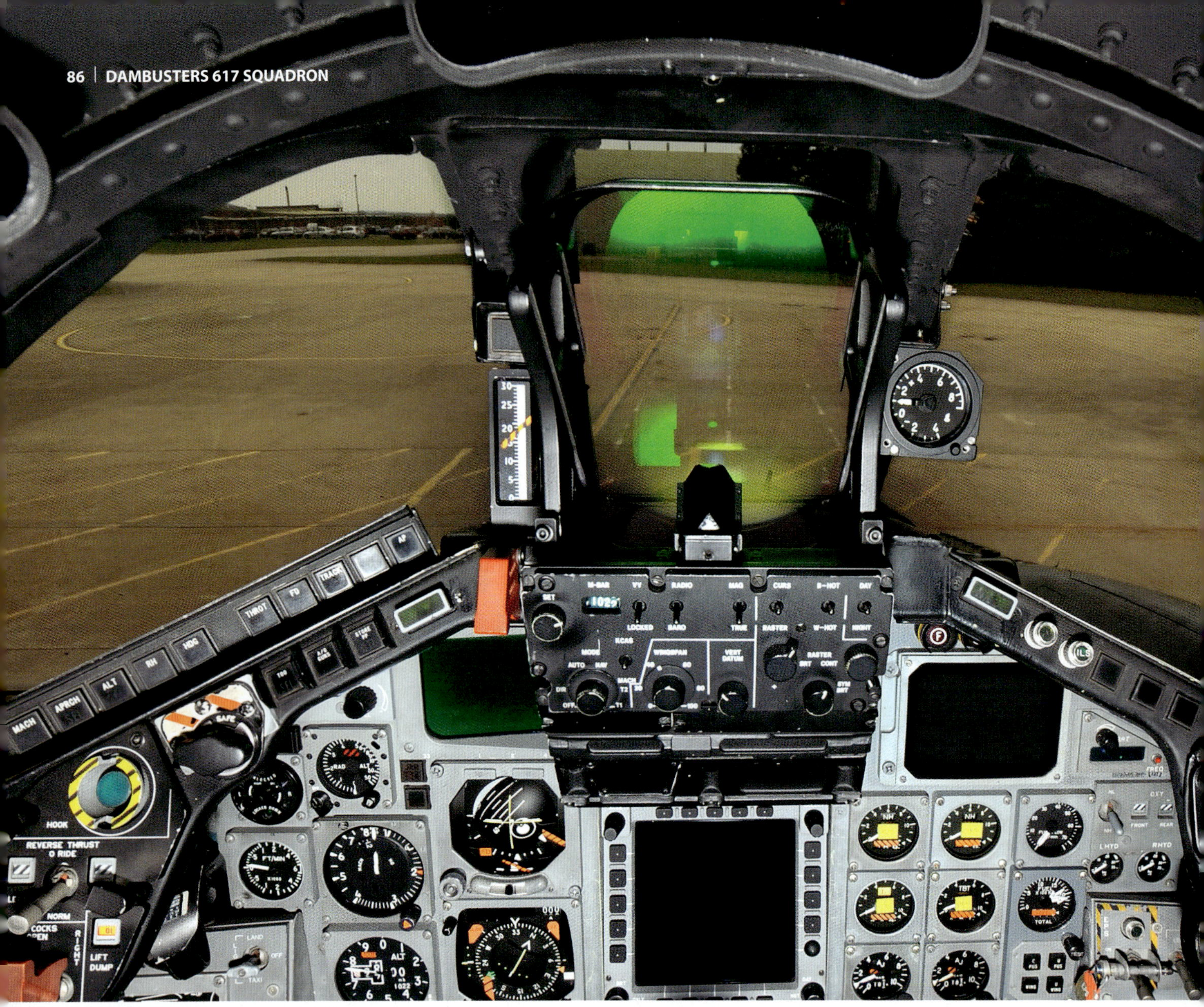
MACH
ALT
HDG
THROT
FD
TRACK
AP
HOOK
REVERSE THRUST
O RIDE
NORM
LIFT
DUMP
SET
RADIO
LOCKED
BARO
TRUE
RASTER
DAY
NIGHT
TOTAL
LHYD
RHYD

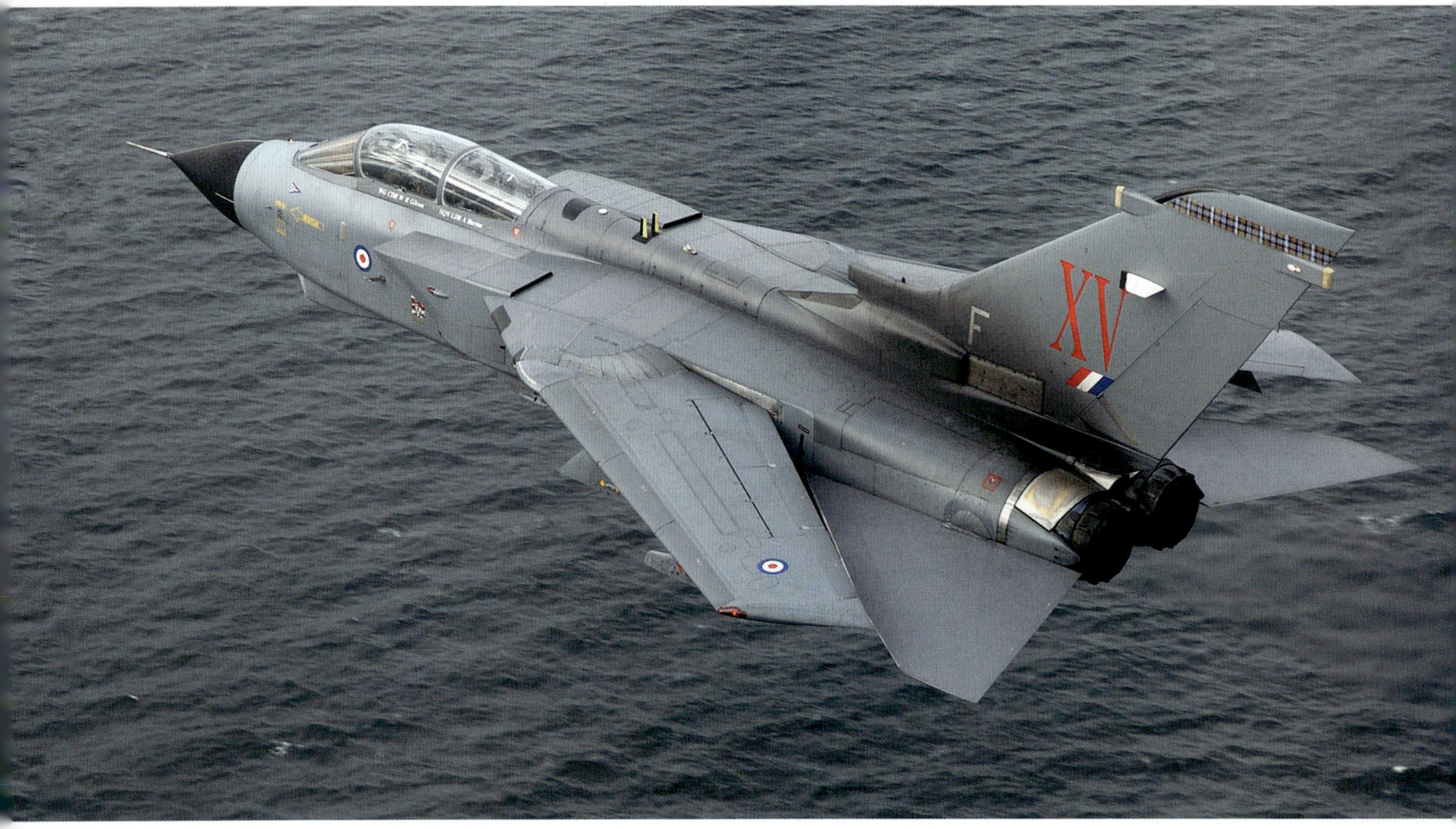
XV
F

The RAF recognised the GR1's exceptional performance and results obtained during the early high-risk, low-level missions, but the realisation that it was essential to use the GR1 at medium altitudes engendered a profound re-examination of the philosophy of Tornado operations and Combat Air capability requirements. The situation encountered during Desert Storm highlighted the need for new weaponry and 'stand-off' capability, which eventually bore fruit with the Storm Shadow missile programme.

With the conclusion of Desert Storm, the GR1 and, later, GR4, became deeply involved in international operations, mainly in the Middle East. Southern and northern no-fly zones were established over Iraq and almost continually patrolled by the Tornado, providing reconnaissance and kinetic effects when required. Repeated rotational deployments to the bases at Incirlik, Turkey, for Operation Warden and to the bases at Al Kharj, Saudi Arabia and Ali Al Salem, Kuwait for Operations Jural, Bolton and Resonate continued until 2009. A significant presence at Al Udeid in Qatar was also maintained until June 2009.

While the majority of sorties during these operations have only included sporadic kinetic events, Operation Desert Fox, a Coalition effort employing Operation Jural assets, included 28 operational Tornado sorties for a total of 48 Paveway II and III LGBs dropped, all of them from medium altitude.

With the Tornado GR1 approaching its Out of Service Date, another mission was assigned to the Brüggen Wing Tornados, which took part in Operation Allied Force over the Balkans in 1999. On April 4, 1999, six Tornado GR1s took off from the German station, in company with four VC10 tankers, for a 7.5-hour round trip to the Balkans; this was the first combat mission flown from an RAF Main Operating Base since World War II and demonstrated the reach and effectiveness of the Tornado. Subsequently, more than 160 combat missions were conducted against targets in Serbia and Kosovo, including missions from Solenzara in Corsica towards the end of the conflict. »

◀ The Tornado GR4 cockpit was upgraded as capabilities evolved. © UK MoD Crown Copyright 2023

◀▼ On April 1, 1992, XV(R) Sqn formed out of the TWCU, which had been using 45 Sqn's 'numberplate' since 1984. Sgt Jack Pritchard, DCC(RAF)/© UK MoD Crown Copyright 2023

▼ Storm Shadow, modelled here by a 617 Sqn GR4, was carried on the outer underfuselage pylons. © UK MoD Crown Copyright 2023

88 | DAMBUSTERS 617 SQUADRON

▼ Preparing to take fuel from a US Air Force tanker over Afghanistan in June 2011, this GR4 has a Litening III pod under its forward fuselage, Brimstone launcher aft and Terma countermeasures pod on its port outer wing pylon. **MSgt William Greer/US Air Force**

▲ Tornado GR4s from 12(B) Squadron took over the Operation Herrick commitment from 1(F) Squadron's Harriers in 2009. This GR4 is armed with Paveway IV PGMs. **SAC Neil Chapman/© UK MoD Crown Copyright 2023**

◄ The Red Flag exercises held out of Nellis Air Force Base, Nevada, provide 'just about the most realistic training you can get without being shot at'. Nellis is on the ouskirts of Las Vegas and the lights of the Strip shine brightly behind this IX(B) Sqn jet in March 2011. **Staff Sgt William P Coleman/US Air Force**

GR4 in Combat

Tension with Iraq escalated again early in 2003 and 32 Tornado GR4s deployed to Ali Al Salem and Al Udeid as part of Operation Telic, within the wider Coalition mission Operation Iraqi Freedom. GR4s flew significant low-level sorties against mobile 'Scud' missile threats and Telic also saw the first use of Storm Shadow as several missiles were launched against high-value targets with great success.

Additionally, 360 Enhanced Paveway II and IIIs (with laser and GPS guidance) were dropped, along with 255 Paveway II and III LGBs. The GR4 also launched 45 ALARMs. Survivability was excellent, although one crew and aircraft were lost to friendly fire. At the end of the conflict, the Tornado remained on overwatch duties in the Gulf, flying RAPTOR missions from Ali Al Salem and then Al Udeid.

On June 14, 2009 the GR4 deployed to Afghanistan for the first time, relieving the Harrier Force on Operation Herrick. Two weeks later, the Tornados returned from Al Udeid, bringing to an end almost 19 years of deployment to the Gulf theatre.

The Tornado GR4 remained engaged in Afghanistan, based at Kandahar Airfield, until November 2014. New capabilities added before the first deployment included a countermeasures pod to defeat infrared »

Tornado Air Defence Variant

In 1971, the RAF's requirement for an interceptor variant of the Tornado IDS was formalised. Such a version had been a possibility from the outset and now the Service was looking for a machine with long range, high speed, powerful radar and a healthy missile load, that could intercept and destroy Soviet bombers when they were still far from reaching the launch points for their long-range missiles. In the Tornado F3 that began replacing its English Electric Lightning and McDonnell Douglas Phantom interceptors from 1987, the RAF got exactly the aircraft it wanted.

BAe began work on two ADV prototypes in 1977. The IDS fuselage was lengthened so that the ADV could accommodate four SkyFlash air-to-air missiles (AAMs), semi-recessed in bays on its underside, while four Sidewinder AAMs were carried under the wings. The aircraft's powerful Foxhunter radar took some time to mature and for a while the interim Tornado F2, which allowed Tornado ADV work-up to begin, flew without radar.

In service, the Tornado F3 was an excellent interceptor and although naturally limited in dogfighting ability, any weaknesses that it may have had were generally compensated for by the use of clever tactics by its well-trained crews. The RAF retired the type in 2011, in favour of Typhoon, the F3 having taken on its fair share of operational commitments, primarily in the Middle East, over the Balkans and on the Falkland Islands.

missile threats, Paveway IV, Dual Mode Seeker (DMS) Brimstone and the installation of Enhanced Common Air Ground Net radios, for effective, secure communications with land forces.

Aircraft software was also updated, to fully exploit the inherent capabilities of the Litening III targeting pod. Additionally performing the intelligence surveillance and reconnaissance (ISR) mission, the pod linked in real-time with joint tactical air controller (JTAC) computer terminals, while the Reconnaissance Airborne Pod Tornado (RAPTOR) provided a stand-off ISR capability and was particularly effective in the change-detection counter-IED (improvised explosive device) mission.

The routine of Tornado deployments was quickly established, the seven frontline squadrons initially moving through Afghanistan on a three-monthly cycle that was subsequently extended slightly to better fit the rotation of ground units. Missions typically employed pairs of jets and were generally launched on a pre-planned basis to deliver close air support (CAS), overwatch and reconnaissance; as more specialised recce missions with one of the two jets carrying RAPTOR; or on a quick reaction alert basis, known as ground close air support (GCAS). Usually launched to a troops-in-contact situation where Coalition ground forces were heavily engaged, two GCAS jets were kept ready for take-off.

▲ A GR4 heads out from RAF Marham alongside a VC10 tanker, during the first Ellamy Storm Shadow mission on March 19, 2011. **SAC Neil Chapman/© UK MoD Crown Copyright 2023**

▲▲ A 13 Sqn GR4 leads an anonymous jet in a formation take-off at RAF Marham in January 2012. Number 13 Squadron is now based at RAF Waddington, operating the Reaper remotely piloted aircraft. **SAC Richard Dudley/© UK MoD Crown Copyright 2023**

▼ RAPTOR was a large store, as demonstrated by this GR4 departing Marham for Gioia del Colle and Operation Ellamy in 2011. The large underwing tanks were a legacy of the F3 fleet. **Cpl Nik Howe/© UK MoD Crown Copyright 2023**

▲ A IX(B) Sqn Tornado GR4 taxies for a mission at Kandahar, on February 15, 2010.
© UK MoD Crown Copyright 2023

▲ In 2012, 41 Sqn painted this Tornado GR4 to commemorate the 1930s' Olympic achievements of former CO Donald Finlay. The jet launched four Storm Shadows on a 2014 test flight over the Atlantic.
Cpl Mark Parkinson/© UK MoD Crown Copyright 2023

A variety of 'effects' could be requested and delivered by the Tornado crews, escalating from the 'show of force', through cannon fire to Brimstone and Paveway IV, so-called kinetic effects. The aim was always to employ the minimum force required for the job in hand.

A show of force was often sufficient to send the enemy into retreat. Continued as a valuable tactic into Operation Shader, it involved a low, fast pass over enemy positions, typically at 100ft and around 500kts, with reheat engaged. Air show goers will be familiar with the spectacle of the low, fast pass, but removed from the crowd for safety's sake. The effect of such a manoeuvre directly overhead is devastating, overwhelming the recipient's senses with a physical wall of otherworldly sound, heat and smell, leaving the air crackling and swirling in the jet's wake.

The Herrick rotations continued until 31 Sqn completed the final deployment, departing Kandahar for Akrotiri on November 11, 2014 and landing back at Marham on November 15. When it despatched its first aircraft and personnel to Afghanistan, the Tornado GR Force had included seven frontline units, II(AC), IX(B), 13 and 31 Sqns at Marham, and 12, 14 and 617 Sqns at Lossiemouth. In June 2011, 13

▲ Two of four Storm Shadows bound for Daesh targets for the first time, on June 26, 2016.
Tony Rogers/© UK MoD Crown Copyright 2023

and 14 Sqns disbanded in accordance with the *2010 Strategic Defence and Security Review*, at a time when TGRF was also committed to Operation Ellamy over Libya.

Operation Ellamy

Libya was already deep into bloody civil war when United Nations Security Council Resolution 1973 was passed on March 17, 2011. Government forces loyal to dictator Colonel Muammar Gaddafi were engaged in a brutal offensive against rebels seeking freedom from decades of repression.

Among other measures, UNSCR 1973 demanded an immediate ceasefire and called for the imposition of a No-Fly Zone over Libya. The latter was instrumental to the resolution's further demand that all measures, barring the insertion of military forces on the ground, should be employed to protect Libyan civilians from harm.

In response, the RAF readied for action under Operation Ellamy, the UK government's contribution to NATO's Operation Unified Protector. Working to keep ahead of the rapidly developing situation, Tornado Force rapidly came to a high state of readiness, in the expectation that Storm Shadow missions might be required from Marham.

In the event, four GR4s, each toting a brace of Storm Shadows, launched as two pairs in the evening of March 19. With VC10 and Tristar tanker support, the Tornados fired their weapons against key command and control facilities exactly on time and with deadly accuracy. The Tristar returned the Tornados to Marham, completing the first RAF strike launched from a UK station since World War II.

During Ellamy's early stages, 12 Sqn was in the process of passing the Herrick commitment to 617 Sqn. The additional tasking over Libya, combined with the demise of two Tornado GR squadrons, then saw 31 Sqn take over from 617 at Kandahar, followed by 12 Sqn and then 617 Sqn again, the latter two units effectively 'pulling double shifts' while II(AC) and IX(B) were embroiled in combat over North Africa.

The 3,000-mile, seven-hour Storm Shadow missions out of Marham inevitably generated media interest, but the reality of on-going deployed operations from Italy was that every Tornado sortie lasted between six and seven hours, involving multiple trips to the tanker and a great deal of loitering on station. The Italy-based Tornados flew alongside Typhoons, for the employment of almost 1,200 weapons over eight months of operations.

Operation Shader

As the Tornado GR Force contracted through 2012 and into 2013, its focus switched temporarily towards contingency and the jet's retirement, but the developing geopolitical situation saw to it that the Tornado's was no quiet work-up to withdrawal. During the night of April 14/15, 2014, Boko Harem, a Nigeria-based extremist terrorist group, kidnapped 276 girls from a government secondary school in Chibok. The international response included a three-Tornado deployment employing RAPTOR as its primary sensor. The aircraft were based in Chad under Operation Turus.

Then, even before 31 Sqn had ended the Herrick commitment, on August 9, 2014, RAF Hercules began dropping supplies to Iraqi civilians forced to take refuge on Mount Sinjar by so-called Islamic State, or Daesh, forces. The flights were performed under Operation Shader, an engagement that became Tornado's primary focus until its withdrawal from combat in January 2019.

▼ Shader missions continued around the clock. This Tornado GR4 has what became the type's classic weapons fit – Paveway IV and DMS Brimstone.
Cpl Sally Raimondo/© UK MoD Crown Copyright 2023

Three Tornados left Marham for Akrotiri on August 13, tasked with providing overwatch and reconnaissance support to the Hercules effort and wider Coalition. On September 26, the House of Commons granted approval for air strikes against Daesh targets in the country and on October 1, two II(AC) Sqn jets destroyed a vehicle with a Paveway IV. Thus, II(AC) Sqn flew Operations Shader and Turus simultaneously during August 2014, while IX(B) took the Herrick commitment and 31 Sqn worked up to replace it.

Meanwhile, 12 Sqn had disbanded on March 1, 2014 and II(AC) Sqn was scheduled to disband early in 2015, but Operation Shader was already looking like a long commitment. Soon, the Tornado and, later, Typhoon squadrons were locked into a constant rotation of personnel between the UK and Akrotiri. It was therefore decided to renumber II(AC)'s Tornado element as a re-formed 12 Sqn at Marham, while the former continued its transition to Typhoon at Lossiemouth. An unusual process, given how recently 12 Sqn had disbanded, it was especially newsworthy because Wg Cdr Nikki Thomas became Officer Commanding 12 Sqn on January 9, 2015; she was the first female commander of an RAF fast jet squadron.

Shader activity had accelerated from December 2, 2014, after the UK government authorised strikes into Syria. The announcement came just days after plans for a revised Tornado withdrawal schedule, with two squadrons to go in 2018 and the last in 2019, were revealed in the *2015 Strategic Defence and Security Review*.

Operations continued at pace for the next 18 months and on July 26, 2016, Storm Shadow was launched against Daesh targets for the first time. Two Tornados fired four weapons that reportedly penetrated deeply into a bunker before detonation. Subsequent strikes made similarly efficient use of the weapon.

Back at home, XV (Reserve) Squadron had taken its final two student aircrew into the last nine-month 'long course' in May 2016; its operational conversion job complete, XV(R) Sqn disbanded on March 31, 2017. Tornado Force simultaneously marked 25 years of continuous operations, finishing a Marham aircraft in the 'desert pink' scheme originally applied to the GR1 for Operation Granby in 1991. Known as 'Pinky', it flew for the first time in its new colours on July 28, 2017.

▲ ZA601/066 lands back from the Tornado's final Shader sortie. Cpl Tim Laurence/© UK MoD Crown Copyright 2023

Contrary to SDSR 2015, two squadrons – IX(B) and 31 – continued through 2018 and into 2019, although from a flying perspective they comprised a single Tornado Force. The situation was somewhat different from an engineering point of view, where keeping IX(B) and 31's requirements separate made for more efficient operations. Defence Secretary Gavin Williamson visited Marham on January 10, 2019 to publicly announce the transfer of Tornado's full offensive capability to Typhoon, while also describing 617 Sqn's Lightnings as operationally ready. Then, on January 31, 2019, the Tornado flew its last ever operational mission; the final Shader jets returned home to Marham from Akrotiri on February 5.

Back at the Norfolk base, three special schemes emerged to mark the end of the Tornado era. Bearing the legend 'IX(B) SQUADRON TORNADO 1982 – 2019', ZG775/AF was marked for the senior Tornado squadron, with a large green bat on its all-black fin. ZD716/DH, painted with '31 SQUADRON TORNADO 1984 – 2019' titles, used the 'Tonka's' ample fin as the canvas for a giant gold star, while the final 'special', ZG752, was repainted in the Dark Sea Grey/Dark Green wraparound camouflage associated with the Cold War-era GR.Mk 1; it also wore the unit badges of every RAF Tornado GR operator.

A three-day series of three-ship flypasts began around the UK on February 19 and although the Tornado was released to service up to March 31, 2019, flying ended on March 14, with a spirited flypast over Marham. Around 850 guests had gathered at the station for the joint disbandment parade of IX(B) and 31 Sqns, also effectively the disbandment of Tornado Force.

▲ The FINale nine-ship (plus a spare) taxies at Marham prior to launch on February 28, 2019. Cpl Lee Matthews/© UK MoD Crown Copyright 2023

MIGHTY EIGHTH
SPECIAL FLYPAST PUBLICATION

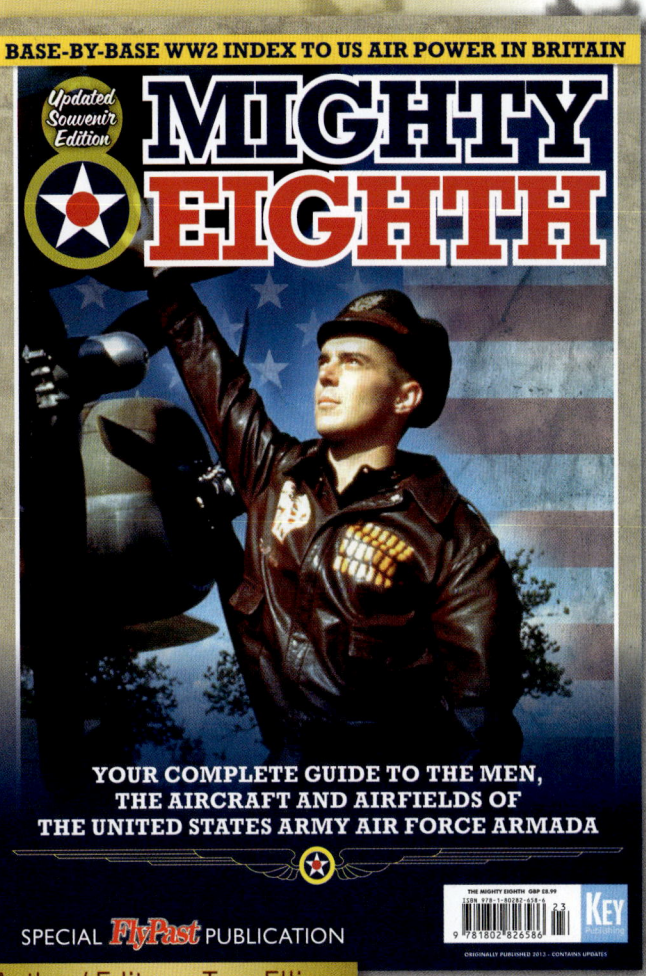

After Pearl Harbor and the US entry into World War Two, priority was given to the war in Europe and American forces poured into the 'unsinkable aircraft carrier' that was Great Britain. From the team behind FlyPast magazine, Mighty Eighth is a 100-page souvenir publication which celebrates the Eighth Air Force – the men, their machines, and the UK airfields they flew from. For the first time, using an innovative base-by-base reference guide, it examines all aspects of American air power in Britain in World War Two and through the 'Cold War'.

Originally published in 2013 and updated for 2023.

100pp

ONLY £8.99 PLUS FREE P&P*

*Free 2nd class P&P on all UK & BFPO orders. Overseas charges apply.

ORDER DIRECT
ALSO AVAILABLE FROM WHSmith AND ALL LEADING NEWSAGENTS

SUBSCRIBERS CALL FOR YOUR £2 DISCOUNT!

Free P&P* when you order online at
shop.keypublishing.com/mightyeighth

OR

Call UK: **01780 480404**
Overseas: **+44 1780 480404**

IF YOU ARE INTERESTED IN THE MIGHTY EIGHTH, YOU MAY ALSO LIKE...

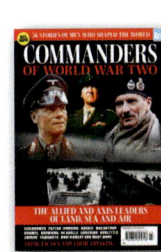

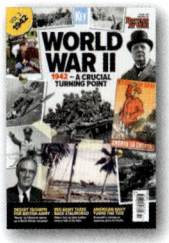
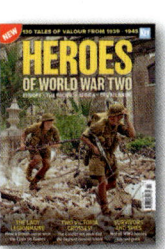

SUBSCRIBE
TO YOUR FAVOURITE MAGAZINE
AND SAVE

Britain at War is dedicated to exploring every aspect of Britain's involvement in conflicts from the turn of the 20th century through to modern day. From World War I to the Falklands, World War II to Iraq, readers are able to re-live decisive moments in Britain's history through fascinating insight combined with rare and previously unseen photography.

shop.keypublishing.com/bawsubs

GREAT SUBSCRIPTION OFFERS FROM

FlyPast is internationally regarded as the magazine for aviation history and heritage. Having pioneered coverage of this fascinating world of 'living history' since 1980, *FlyPast* still leads the field today. Subjects regularly profiled include British and American aircraft type histories, as well as those of squadrons and units from World War One to the Cold War.

shop.keypublishing.com/fpsubs

Aeroplane traces its lineage back to the weekly The Aeroplane launched in June 1911, and is still continuing to provide the best aviation coverage around. *Aeroplane* magazine is dedicated to offering the most in-depth and entertaining read on all historical aircraft.

shop.keypublishing.com/amsubs

Order direct or subscribe at:
shop.keypublishing.com

Or call **UK 01780 480404** Overseas **+44 1780 480404**
Lines open 9.00-5.30, Monday-Friday

THE DAMBUSTERS Today

Based at RAF Marham, Norfolk, 617 Squadron will remain as the UK's frontline F-35B Lightning unit until 809 Naval Air Squadron stands up later this year. Officer Commanding 617 Sqn, Wing Commander Stew Campbell has a unique perspective on the 80th anniversary year, having been involved in the 70th anniversary commemorations in 2013

On March 28, 2014, the Dambusters disbanded as a Tornado unit. Already nominated as the UK's first frontline Lockheed Martin F-35B Lightning II operator, the squadron began preparations for its re-formation in April 2017, when OC-designate Wing Commander John Butcher began the process at a ceremony at the Smithsonian National Air and Space Museum in Washington, DC. He was temporarily based with other squadron members at Marine Corps Air Station Beaufort, South Carolina, where the first cadre of UK F-35 operators was training with Marine Fighter Attack Training Squadron 501 (VMFAT-501) 'Warbirds'. The squadron formally stood up again on April 18, 2018.

On June 6, 2018, Butcher led four Lightnings to RAF Marham, the type's UK main operating base. Their arrival marked the return of 617 Sqn to the station it had called home for almost 12 of its many Tornado years. Marham's first Lightning sortie followed on June 28, with Butcher at the controls, and another five jets arrived on August 3 – the Dambusters were back and like never before.

Since the F-35 had been procured as a joint Royal Air Force and Royal Navy asset, the new 617 Sqn was staffed by personnel from both services. They proved their mettle less than a year later, when Dambusters' jets departed Marham for RAF Akrotiri under Lightning Dawn. From there they exercised with Israeli, Italian and US F-35s, and flew combat sorties over Iraq and Syria, albeit without expending ordnance.

Again, in accordance with its joint staffing, a Royal Navy officer replaced Wg Cdr Butcher at the end of his posting on April 2, 2020. It was therefore Commander Mark Sparrow who led five 617 Sqn Lightnings out to HMS *Queen Elizabeth* during October 2020.

▲ Wing Commander Stew Campbell, Officer Commanding 617 Squadron. **Cpl Hazel Reader/© UK MoD Crown Copyright 2023**

Eight days of training in the North Sea saw UK crews working alongside personnel from Marine Fighter Attack Squadron 211 (VMFA-211) 'Wake Island Avengers' aboard the new carrier. The work-up helped prepare pilots and engineers for embarked operations ahead of Carrier Strike Group 21 (CSG21), an international cruise by HMS *Queen Elizabeth* and its strike group during which the vessel and its fast jet complement would be tested under operational conditions through the Mediterranean and far out into the Pacific.

The aircraft carrier sailed from Portsmouth on May 1, 2021, its embarked 617 Sqn and VMFA-211 F-35Bs taking part in Exercise Strike Warrior off Scotland between May 8 and 19. After a brief period in port, the carrier strike group formed up around HMS *Queen Elizabeth* after it left Portsmouth again »

Sitting under one of Marham's purpose-built shelters, this F-35B was being prepared for a Red Flag exercise in 2020. The structure to the left in the background is one of the station's remaining hardened aircraft shelters. **SAC Kitty Barratt/© UK MoD Crown Copyright 2023**

on May 22. Multiple exercises with aircraft and ships from countries all along its route continued into October, when the force began its return leg to the UK. Back in British waters, 617 Sqn flew its F-35Bs off the carrier as the entire force returned to base during December, albeit one Lightning had been lost in November owing to a maintenance anomaly; the pilot ejected safely. That one incident notwithstanding, CSG21 had proven the capability of ship and Lightning, and the Dambusters' ability to conduct embarked operations.

Towards 80

The squadron therefore entered 2022 in good shape as thoughts turned to the 80th anniversary of its formation and most famous operation. After a brief tenure in command, Wg Cdr Tait made way for Wg Cdr Stew Campbell who, in early April 2023, was in his fourth year on the unit, having already served as executive officer, or XO, effectively second in command. He is acutely aware of the anniversary's significance, having been a squadron member in 2013 and responsible for the series of flying appearances that marked the 70th anniversary.

Campbell left 617 Sqn for the Red Arrows, displaying from 2014 to 2016, before going to Lightning Force Headquarters in January 2017, first as deputy chief of staff and then in a pilot training role. Now, his office on

▲ The F-35's cockpit is especially distinctive for its lack of head-up display. Critical mission data is instead displayed directly onto the helmet visor. **Cpl Amy Lupton/© UK MoD Crown Copyright 2023**

▶ Life aboard ship is becoming second nature to 617 Sqn's RAF contingent, while their Royal Navy colleagues have probably never felt more at home. **AS1 Natalie Adams/© UK MoD Crown Copyright 2023**

the second floor of the still-new Lightning complex overlooks the flightline, where the jets sit under shelters as they typically might at a US base.

The squadron building at Lossiemouth was crammed with memorabilia, while its basic fabric might have been on any UK RAF station at any time since the late 1930s. The Dambusters' Marham home is quite different, but nonetheless manages to feel special. Memorabilia is collected into display cabinets and fine artwork decorates the walls, including extraordinary paintings of Lancasters and dams, and Lightnings and aircraft carriers. A series of planform silhouettes of the squadron's aircraft decorating the walls of the stairwell is an especially nice touch.

Campbell believes the Dambusters' heritage is as important to today's unit members as it ever has been. "The part of that I find most pleasing is the pride the squadron's Royal Navy personnel have in being on 617 Sqn. I try to interview everyone when they leave the squadron and while I'd kind of assumed it from the RAF personnel, when I ask about people's highlights almost everyone says it was being a Dambuster. And no one has left for a promotion course who hasn't wanted to come back."

Although the 80th anniversary events are less overt than in 2013, from his unique personal perspective Campbell says they are equally significant. "We had a dining-in night and six of us went up to Scampton church to see a new stained glass window installed.

The only downside for the squadron is that just as we were in 2013, we'll be deployed on exercise in May – it was Al Minhad in 2013 and it'll be North America this time."

Ships and Squadrons

Today's 617 Sqn is very different to its 2013 incarnation. The unit has a long association with ships, one in which its aircraft were rarely welcome. That changed with the F-35B and although flying a fast jet onto an aircraft carrier seems extraordinary from the outside, Campbell reckons it is something 617's RAF and Royal Navy pilots are barely concerned with until their first deployment. "Even then, it's generally a positive experience. I really enjoy going in the ship, especially on shorter deployments, because we tend to fly a lot and »

▲ In the years since World War II, the sky around Marham has reverberated to the sound of Washington, Canberra and Valiant bombers, Victor inflight refuelling tankers, the Tornado and, today, the Lightning. The station's infrastructure was transformed ahead of the fifth-generation jet's arrival.
Cpl Pippa Fowles/© UK MoD Crown Copyright 2023

▲ The setting sun highlights the transparent sensor window under the F-35's nose. It covers elements of the aircraft's electro-optical targeting system, part of an integrated suite of sensors that means the Lightning has no need to carry external targeting pods. **AS1 Natalie Adams/© UK MoD Crown Copyright 2023**

go to different places almost every day, rather than deploying to a single operating base."

The Dambusters are not alone in operating the F-35 at Marham since 207 Sqn, the Lightning operational conversion unit, is already at the station and 809 Naval Air Squadron will reform there this year. Looking beyond Marham, but not too far away in Suffolk, there are more Lightnings, F-35As with the US Air Force's 495th Fighter Squadron (FS) 'Valkyries' at RAF Lakenheath. The close working relationship Campbell describes with the US unit befits the 80th anniversary year – American pilot Flt Lt Joe McCarthy was responsible for delivering an Upkeep weapon against the Sorpe dam.

"We work very closely together," Campbell enthuses. "We're flying with them today and over the past couple of weeks almost every other day. We've visited Lakenheath for social events and hosted 'Valkyries' personnel here. We're working on making the relationship as close as possible, building on the fact that F-35s can talk to one another. The closer we are to our F-35 allies, the better we can fight together."

Compared to 2013, the Dambusters are marking their 80th anniversary on a new jet at a different base. In terms of capability and personnel, the squadron has been transformed. And yet some traditions remain. A decade ago, it was seen as very poor form for a squadron member not to have a DVD of *The Dam Busters* movie from 1955 prominently placed for easy watching. How has the tradition survived in the face of streaming services?

"This is a reference to our so-called TacEval," Campbell laughs. "The TacEval, or tactical evaluation, was a Cold War assessment of squadron operations that has turned into a 617 Sqn social tradition where the unit's junior officers 'TacEval' more senior officers by arranging with their partners to arrive unannounced at their home, expecting to be entertained. That entertainment must include having *The Dam Busters* on the TV as soon as possible.

We have it paid for on Prime. I've been 'TacEvaled' twice and the second time my wife had it on pause ready to go so I just needed to press play!"

Wing Commander Campbell flew two Herrick tours as a Tornado pilot during his first association with the Dambusters and now commands the RAF's most famous squadron flying the service's first fifth-generation combat aircraft. Is it possible, through that combat and command experience, to imagine flying a Lancaster at low level, deep into occupied territory to deliver an experimental weapon against a well defended target in the dead of night?

"I find it difficult to draw any real comparisons to the bravery of those crews. The only comparison I have is that although our aircraft are single seat, so we don't have a crew, we do fly in formations, and we utterly rely on each other, whether we're training or fighting. Everyone has to be the best they can possibly be, and we hope that if we are called upon, we'll demonstrate similar courage."

SPECIAL MAGAZINES
Essential reading from Key Publishing

SAS
(THE REAL LIFE ROGUE HEROES)
This special publication has been re-released to celebrate the new BBC drama SAS: Rogue Heroes.

£8.99 inc FREE P&P*

P47 THUNDERBOLT
One of the true immortals of World War II is celebrated in this 116 page special.

£8.99 inc FREE P&P*

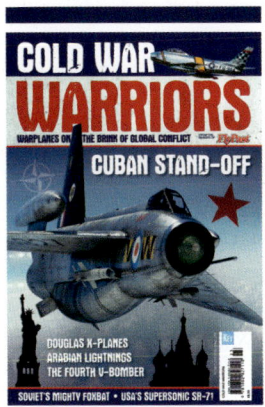

COLD WAR WARRIORS
The Avro Vulcan, the Boeing B-47 Stratojet, the English Electric Lightning, the MiG-25 Foxbat and the awesome Lockheed SR-71 Blackbird.

£8.99 inc FREE P&P*

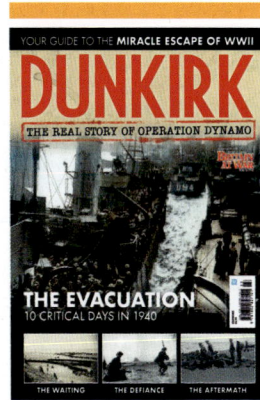

DUNKIRK
The operation known as 'Dunkirk' was referred to as the 'Phoney War' but ended with 300,000 men being saved to fight another day.

£8.99 inc FREE P&P*

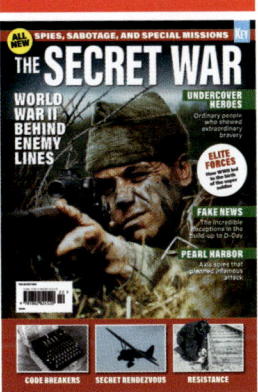

THE SECRET WAR:
Espionage and Special Operations in World War Two

£8.99 inc FREE P&P*

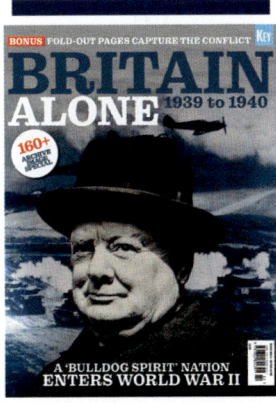

BRITAIN ALONE 1939-40
This is a reissue of The War Archives World War II – Britain Alone 1939/40, previously published in 2014.

£5.00 inc FREE P&P*

HISTORIC AVIATION YEARBOOK
Packed with fantastic flying heritage, the Historic Aviation Yearbook 2022 brings together the best of market-leading magazines FlyPast and Aeroplane.

£8.99 inc FREE P&P*

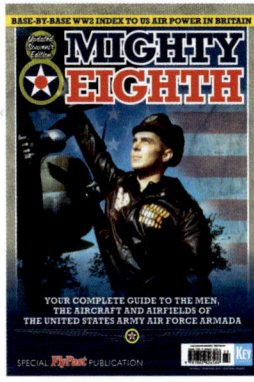

THE MIGHTY EIGHTH
This examines all aspects of American air power in Britain in World War Two.

£8.99 inc FREE P&P*

HOW TO ORDER

 (+44)1780 480404

 shop.keypublishing.com/specials

Also available to download – search **'Aviation Specials'**
on Pocketmags.com or your native app store

*Prices correct at time of going to press. Free 2nd class P&P on all UK & BFPO orders. Overseas charges apply. Postage charges vary depending on total order value.

FIFTH GENERATION Dambusters

Today, the Dambusters operate the fifth-generation, stealthy F-35B Lightning. The aircraft brings a step change in capability, as Officer Commanding 617 Sqn, Wing Commander Stew Campbell explains.

The UK operates its Lockheed Martin F-35B Lightning force out of purpose-built facilities, with an 'enclave' including a squadron building and Integrated Training Centre (ITC) erected in an area of RAF Marham's expansive real estate previously occupied by Cold War hardened aircraft shelters. The ITC houses a spectrum of training devices, including four networked full mission simulators. The Lightning Operations Centre and Maintenance and Finishing facility are located elsewhere across the airfield.

Simulation, or synthetic training, is key to Lightning capability. In the more distant past, pilots used the simulator for recurrent training and practising techniques that were less safe to explore in the air. Emergency drills were typically repeated in the simulator, for example, but modern devices are a world away in capability and fidelity. The UK's Lightning pilots complete 50% of their training in the simulator, either in Marham's dedicated training facility or one of its mobile systems, which may be embarked in HMS *Queen Elizabeth* or HMS *Prince of Wales*.

Equipped to simulate the full range of mission capability – and for practising emergency procedures – the Lightning simulators enable training that would otherwise

◀ The F-35B's airframe is transformed in the transition from wingborne to slow speed or vertical flight and back again. As the aircraft slows, large doors in the forward centre fuselage open to admit air to the Rolls-Royce lift fan and Pratt & Whitney F135 engine, while the exhaust nozzle rotates vertically downwards at the rear. **POPhot Jay Allen/© UK MoD Crown Copyright 2023**

be impossible during peacetime. They are also used for the conversion of pilots onto the F-35 since there are no two-seat Lightnings. Officer Commanding 617 Sqn, Wing Commander Stew Campbell explains: "We practise high-end tactics in the simulator that we can't do for real in training for security reasons, and the simulator just keeps on getting better. In 40 years' time, I believe the building, just like the jet, will look the same on the outside as it does now, but on the inside, I won't recognise it."

Every effort is made to keep the simulators on a par with and ideally ahead of the latest aircraft software standard so that pilots are familiar with changes before they go flying. Marham's simulators are networked so that four may be 'flown' together on the same 'mission'. Beyond that, Campbell sees off-base networking, initially with other F-35s, as the next major progression. "It's a big piece of work that's being done now and hopefully, in time, it will allow us to link in to an even wider network."

Simulation also plays an important role in preparing pilots for embarked operations. It is used in combination with real-world flying, for which 617 Sqn is returning to sea later in 2023. Two levels of ship simulation are available, at Marham and BAE Systems'

Warton site in Lancashire, where the fidelity of the ship itself is much higher. "BAE Systems built its simulator to help with designing the aircraft carrier. They needed to understand how the superstructure would affect wind over the deck and how that would affect the jet. So, it was designed as an aid for the shipbuilders and now we use it for really accurate training because the modelling is so accurate. The 'sim' here at Marham has the ship in it but doesn't have the detailed wind modelling. The simulations are spot on in terms of the ship's stability – you aren't really aware of it moving, especially when you're alongside."

Working week

Asked to define a typical flying day or working week on 617 Sqn, Campbell jokingly responds that for the OC there is no such concept, but ideally pilots fly the jet and the 'sim' twice each, every week. "A flight or sim takes up most of the day, especially if its higher level tactical training. Then everyone also has secondary duties and the best part of a day to gather thoughts and prepare for the next week."

Back in 1943, each of the dams raid Lancasters flew with a crew of seven: pilot, navigator, bomb aimer, wireless (radio) operator, flight engineer, front gunner, and rear gunner. The single pilot of an F-35 is effectively responsible for the tasks of all those individually trained crew. He or she

▲ Inflight refuelling is a critical element in most missions, training and operational. Here two Lightnings hold off the Voyager tanker's drogues while a Typhoon flies alongside.
Cpl Alex Scott/© UK MoD Crown Copyright 2023

▼ The Dambusters deployed to Nellis Air Force Base, Nevada, for Exercise Red Flag 20-1 in February 2020.
Cpl Amy Lupton/© UK MoD Crown Copyright 2023

▲ In November 2022, the Dambusters were back aboard HMS *Queen Elizabeth* as part of Operation Achillean, a proof-of-concept deployment of maritime strike capability, comprising F-35s, and Merlin and Wildcat helicopters. **AS1 Adams/© UK MoD Crown Copyright 2023**

flies the jet, including taking care of all the basic requirements essential to safe operations, navigates, prosecutes the target, communicates (through radio and data link), monitors aircraft systems and takes responsibility for its defence against enemy action. How are individuals trained in this complex skillset? And how are their skills kept sharp in peacetime in the knowledge that tomorrow or the next day they may have to do it all for real?

Campbell explains: "We have a very structured training programme run by two instructor pilots. It cycles through all the mission sets we're declared to hold, with exercises fed in. In March we flew an exercise with USAFE [US Air Forces Europe] also involving the Norwegians and Dutch, and early in April we flew with multiple RAF Typhoon squadrons and Lakenheath jets out over the North Sea, in preparation for an exercise in North America next month.

"When we come back from that, we'll reset, then look at areas where we've not trained for a little while, after which our attention will be on preparations for returning to the ship. We're constantly working through the training cycle."

Individuals arrive on the squadron as junior wingmen and Campbell's aim is for all to progress and become four-ship leaders before the end of their tour. "After that, they may re-tour on 617 Sqn, go to the qualified weapons »

▼ In March 2022, 617 Sqn deployed to Amari Air Base, Estonia for a period of enhanced Vigilance Activity in the Baltic region as a contribution to NATO's increased presence following Russia's invasion of Ukraine. **Cpl Egan/© UK MoD Crown Copyright 2023**

▶ The F-35B delivers its unique capability equally well from ship or shore. This was a night launch during Operation Achillean.
LPhot Belinda Alker/© UK MoD Crown Copyright 2023

instructor course or become an instructor on the OCU," he notes.

Later in the aircraft's career, the Tornado squadrons had worked in a similar way, generally rotating through mission sets in between preparations for deployment, but there are fundamental differences between the 'Tonka' and the Lightning. Campbell enthuses: "We have more mission sets than Tornado and it's important to highlight that the Lightning is much more capable. It's lightyears ahead of Tornado. Our ability to switch through mission sets is seamless and we need to remain proficient in doing that, but the jet's capability is second to none."

The post-mission debrief is a critical element of any training sortie. Where 617 has trained alongside US F-35s or F-15Es and Typhoons in a single mission, for example, the participating aircraft likely land back at Marham, Lakenheath, Coningsby and even Lossiemouth. Given the need for enhanced security where the F-35 and its capabilities are concerned, various techniques are employed to bring crews together over what might be considerable distances.

"After we've flown with the 495th FS F-35s we sometimes drive to Lakenheath for face-to-face debrief and sometimes land there, debrief, then fly home. We also use a 'secret' phone system and, one level up from that, a secret video conferencing system that links between the US and all UK bases and, as we proved last year, Norway. But the best is always face-to-face because that's how you really understand one another's problems, strengths, and weaknesses."

Landing the F-35 away from Marham is possible so long as a suitable runway is available, but the jet's peculiar requirement generates what Campbell terms a 'fairly significant security footprint'. "If we pre-position our security force we can go anywhere and we have a team ready to react if we have to divert. Going to places like Lakenheath, Coningsby or Lossiemouth is easier because of the security they already have in place."

Air-to-air

Compared to the Tornado GR4 and, indeed, the dedicated Tornado F3 air defender, the F-35B has a formidable air-to-air capability. It is important around the ship, where the jet extends the defensive shield around the carrier strike group out to several hundred miles, and 617 Sqn's regular training is biased towards it; F-35B pilots are expected to take care of aerial threats even during a strike mission. Flying air-to-air is tough mentally and physically, so what does a former Tornado GR4 pilot make of it?

"It's something the squadron practises every day. The difference is whether we're in a defensive counter-air mindset as we would be on the carrier or offensive mindset, which would be us going forward. The young pilots enjoy it, but I find it more challenging. The jet helps by providing a huge amount of situational awareness.

"The TOPGUN style of close-in dogfighting, which is often and arguably described as the most fun you can have in a fighter jet, is something we do less regularly than the Typhoon squadrons. Much of our air-to-air war is like a game of chess played from quite a significant distance."

The F-35 is, of course, stealthy, which from the outside begs the question of why it would need to engage enemy aircraft at all. Campbell is candid in response. "Stealth isn't an invisibility cloak. It's built around

▲ The Dambusters embarked for their first ever carrier operations in September 2020, ahead of the Carrier Strike Group 21 deployment. **LPhot Luke/© UK MoD Crown Copyright 2023**

◀ Contrary to some reports, the F-35B offers a rugged operating capability, albeit with a few unique maintenance requirements. This jet was being de-iced prior to a mission from Amari in March 2022. **SAC Ben Mayfield/© UK MoD Crown Copyright 2023**

▼ Although the F-35B's advanced flight control system enables 'push button landings' from alongside the ship, pilots must still be aware of the hazards posed by wind over the deck and around the superstructure, and the hot efflux trailing in the ship's wake from its funnel. **LPhot Unaisi Luke/© UK MoD Crown Copyright 2023**

the concept of stopping us being shot down, not necessarily preventing an enemy knowing we are there. It's impossible to hide completely."

Talking together

Collaboration between F-35 operators is fundamental to how the aircraft works. Campbell and his counterpart at the 495th FS coordinate training opportunities between Marham's F-35Bs and the USAFE F-35As at nearby RAF Lakenheath. Beyond that, Campbell enthuses: "It's no secret we don't have a huge number of F-35s, but many countries are buying it and the way it works is effectively by talking to one another and fighting together. So, the closer we are to the F-35 units in Italy, the Netherlands, Norway, the US and other nations, the better. If called upon, we'll fight together."

In May 1943, 617 Sqn sent 19 Lancasters deep into enemy territory. They were expected to avoid detection by flying low, fight their way in and out again as necessary, and deliver a weapon with pinpoint accuracy, all with no support. Today's RAF aims to fight cooperatively with its own assets or those of its allies, and although the F-35 might be the spearhead in a peer or near-peer conflict, 617 Sqn would not expect to go to war alone.

As part of a joint attacking force with Typhoon, therefore, the F-35 might fly ahead to engage and neutralise surface-to-air missile (SAM) threats, creating a safe 'corridor' through which heavily armed Typhoons could penetrate deeper into contested airspace.

Together, Lightning and Typhoon are far more effective than either platform alone, while both are subject to an ongoing campaign of improvement. Campbell provides a little detail on how they work together and how the squadrons keep up with the evolving capabilities of one another's platforms.

"We would want to go to war with Typhoon. The F-35 excels in integrating with fourth-generation fighters, including F-15, F-18, F-16, and Typhoon. In a UK package it will always be Typhoon and we train for that regularly. Typhoon can go very high and very fast, and it carries a lot more ordnance than us, but with our sensors and radar we can see a lot more.

"Exactly how a mission is flown depends very much on the threat. Our team would analyse it and determine suitable tactics. There are two options if we are looking to defeat an air defence system, destroy it or suppress it – we can drop a bomb on it or use the radar for electronic attack and suppress it. The choice would be tactics driven. If there were enemy aircraft in the way, we'd get rid of those too."

In 1943, the Dambusters relied on pre-war maps and photographs taken by camera-equipped Spitfires for pre-raid intelligence and damage assessment. A detailed knowledge of the target and enemy defences is just as important today, but the means of gathering intelligence is dramatically different. High-resolution satellite imagery has replaced the need to overfly the target, the internet provides a plethora of information, and »

▶ Lightning pilots have several choices of how to take-off or land. This conventional take-off was from RAF Marham. **SAC Natalie Adams/© UK MoD Crown Copyright 2023**

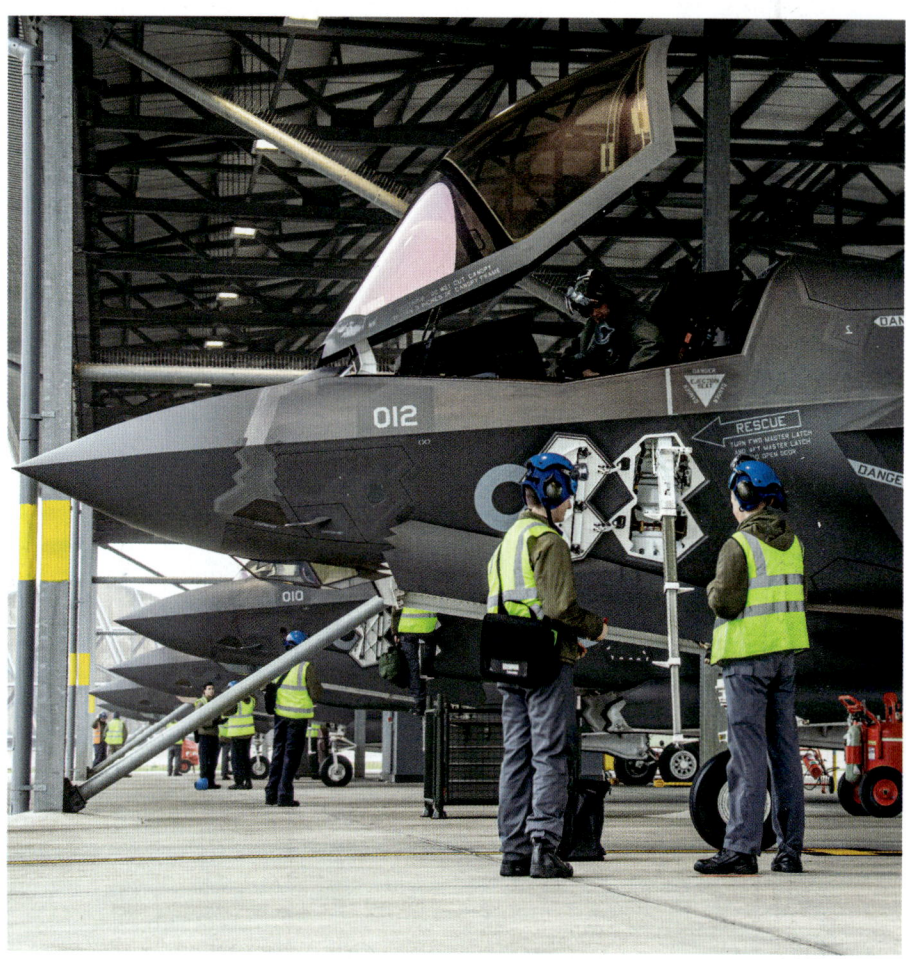

platforms, including Rivet Joint and other than electromagnetic spectrum, revealing frequencies and communications networks vital to military planning. It should also be remembered that the Lightning, especially, 'soaks up' gigabytes of data through its sensor system and therefore represents a formidable ISR platform itself.

"There can still be an element of surprise though," Campbell cautions. "SAM systems can move, and smart operators don't turn them on until they need to, so although we have a lot of information beforehand and the jet is phenomenal at piecing together the battlespace as you progress, we still prepare for the unexpected; if a radar isn't turned on, the jet can't see it.

"The aircraft is all about warfighting, with systems that relieve the pilot's workload and allow them to think about the battlespace. I'd say that around 20% of a pilot's ability is required to fly the F-35, leaving 80% to fight it. But there is still a huge amount of information that has to be handled carefully to avoid saturation, and there are still ways to make mistakes or get into trouble. I'd say in many ways it is more straightforward to fly than a Tornado. It's easier from a control perspective but tactically more complex. It requires a very different skillset.

"I'm very content that the UK bought the right aircraft with F-35. I firmly believe it's the best multirole fighter in the world, with its ability to switch between mission sets so quickly. The F-22 has the edge on us air-to-air,

▲ Numbers 207 and 617 Sqns deployed aircraft for Exercise Red Flag 20-1. In this January 22, 2020 photo, RAF Marham's shelters provide protection as pilots prepare for the long transatlantic crossing. **SAC Kitty Barratt/© UK MoD Crown Copyright 2023**

▲ Number 617 Sqn would choose to go into battle alongside the Typhoon. As this jet departing for a 2021 Operation Shader mission demonstrates, the Typhoon can carry a considerable load of ordnance and other stores. **Cpl Lee Matthews/© UK MoD Crown Copyright 2023**